PARTICLE ZEN

AND THE
LIFE SCIENCE OF BECOMING NO THING

SCOTT SHAW

BUDDHA ROSE PUBLICATIONS

Particle Zen and the Life Science of Becoming No Thing
Copyright © 2020 By Scott Shaw
www.scottshaw.com
All Rights Reserved

Cover Photographs By Scott Shaw
Copyright © 2020 All Rights Reserved
Rear Cover Photograph of Scott Shaw By Hae Won Shin
Copyright © 2020 All Rights Reserved.

This book contains material protected under International and Federal Copyright Laws and Treaties. Any unauthorized reprint or use of this material is prohibited. No part of this book may be reproduced or transmitted in any form or by any means, electronic or mechanical, including photocopying, recording, or by any information storage and retrieval system without express written permission from the author or publisher.

First Edition 2020
ISBN 10: 1-949251-30-6
ISBN 13: 978-1-949251-30-2
Library of Congress: 2020939560

Printed in the United States of America
10 9 8 7 6 5 4 3 2

PARTICLE ZEN
AND THE LIFE SCIENCE OF BECOMING NO THING

Introduction

Here it is, *The Scott Shaw Zen Blog 16.0,* originally presented on the *World Wide Web*. All of the writings presented in this book were written between February and May of 2020.

As was the case with the previously published volumes based upon *The Scott Shaw Zen Blog;* entitled: *Scribbles on the Restroom Wall, The Chronicles: Zen Ramblings from the Internet, Words in the Wind, Zen Mind Life Thoughts, The Zen of Life, Lies and Aberrant Reality, Apostrophe Zen, The Abstract Arsenal of Zen and the Psychology of Being, Zen and Again: The Metaphysical Philosophy of Psychology, Tempest in a Teapot and the Den of Zen, Buddha in the Looking Glass, Wo Ton' of the Blue Vision, Zen and the Psychology of the Spiritual Something, Pyrophoric Zen, Fragments of Paradox, Zen: Traversing the Entity of Non-Entity,* and *Zen and the Ambient Echo: The Psychological Philosophy of Being* this volume is presented exactly as it was viewed on *scottshaw.com* with no rewriting, punctuation, or typo corrections. From this, we hope you will receive the original reading experience.

This volume of internet ramblings is presented with the date and time listed as to when each blog was originally posted. Also, the blogs in this volume are presented from last to first. With this, we hope to present a transcendence back through time as opposed to an evolving evolution. In addition, we left out the traditional *Table of Contents* in an attempt to leave this volume with a much more free-flowing reading experience.

Okay, there's the information and the definitions. Read on… We hope you enjoy it. And, be sure to stayed tuned for the ongoing *Scott Shaw Zen Blog @ scottshaw.com.*

You Can't Give Enlightenment to a Person
26/May/2020 06:57 AM

You can't give enlightenment to a person. You can want them to be better. You can hope that they will become better. You can point them in the direction of illumination. You can even tell them what they should do to meet nirvana but if they do not take the steps to reach enlightenment on their own they will never find it.

There are many religious throughout the world but enlightenment has nothing to do with religion. Enlightenment is about entering into a space of cross-dimensional rightness.

Religions want people to join their conclave. Religion wants people to believe as they do. But, belief is easy. It takes no effort. It takes no action. Enlightenment, on the other hand, witnesses a person consciously letting go of the things that hold them bound to karma. The pathway to illumination witnesses the person not doing things that create karma.

Like I have long said, *"Enlightenment is easy, it's life that's hard."* Yet, very few people get it. Moreover, even less care about it.

The reason life is hard is because there are all of these people doing all of these things that get in the way of other people's pathway to enlightenment. There are all of these people doing all of these things that are solely based on how they view the world, how they view other people, what they want from other people, and how they want the world to be. From this, they not only create all kinds of karma in their own life but they set about on a path that places roadblocks in the pathway of other people and hinders them from reaching their full potential. Some people even take joy in this. Explain this to them and they will deny it, they will justify their actions, or they simply will not care. Thus, not only do they hinder other people from reaching their highest goals but they create a barrier from them meeting their own enlightenment.

"Enlightenment is easy, it's life that's hard," and this is the root cause of the problem and why so few people ever reach illumination. Life gets in the way.

There is one person who keeps anyone from reaching enlightenment and that is the person themselves. If you allow other people to do things that keep you from meeting cosmic bliss, if you allow their words or their actions to take control of your mind, then you have allowed them to keep you from encountering your true ultimate nature.

The Bodhisattva Vow details that the true zealot will continue to reincarnate to help humanity until all reach enlightenment. Nice thought, but you cannot feed a person a glass of spiritual emancipation if they are not willing to drink the elixir. Most people are not. They are far too locked up in whatever it is they are thinking about, whatever it is they are desiring, to allow themselves to encountering illumination. Thus, you can't give enlightenment to a person.

So, where dose this leave us? As in all Life Things, it leaves us with you. What do you want? Do you want to touch the divine essence of the all and the everything or do you simply want to be lost to the emotions of the world delivered to you by other people?

"Enlightenment is easy, it's life that's hard." But, you have to choose to make the choice to focus on the something more rather than meaningless momentary reality if you hope to encounter it.

* * *

24/May/2020 12:00 PM

How much did your last mistake cost you?

Most People Don't Want To Admit When They're Wrong
22/May/2020 12:19 PM

Most people don't want to admit when they're wrong. Think about it... Think about all the people who have said something about somebody or something that was untruthful, highly slanted by opinion, or was just flat out wrong. They said it. It was not the truth. Yet, they never did anything to retract their statement. In fact, in many cases, they fought to make their false statement believed by as many people as possible. How about you? Have you ever done that?

There are a million reasons why people want to say something about someone or something. There are millions of opinions in the world. There are those people who wish to broadcast what they think to others.

Some people listen and believe everything they hear. Others scrutinize the words of others and separate the fact from the opinion. Whatever the case, a lot of people say a lot of things. Sometimes the things they are saying are designed to help. Sometimes what they are stating is designed to hurt. But, whatever a person says is based upon nothing more than their own personal interpretation of a subject matter. But, because they believe what they are saying to be true, they feel others should believe as they do. But, should they?

Think about your life. Think about the things you have stated about someone or something. Do you ever question why you are saying what you are saying before you say it? Do your ever question your motivations for saying it in the first place? Do you ever analyze the affect of what you are saying will have on that someone or something else? Do you care? Or, do you only think what you think and that's all you think?

Once you have answered those questions think about what has been the implications of what you have said. Did it help someone or something? Did it hurt someone or something?

How do you feel about that reaction to your action? Is what occurred what you had hoped for? But, more importantly, what was your motivation for saying what you said in the first place? If it was designed to help, why did you want to help that someone or something? If it was deigned to hurt, why did you want to hurt that someone or something? More importantly, what gives you the right to unleash any opinion-based statement onto anyone or anything in the first place? What makes you judge and jury?

Most people operate from a space of what they think is right. But, is it? Have you ever taken the time to truly try to change your mind?

Sometimes change of mind is forced upon us. We are confronted with facts that we cannot deny. But, most of the time this is not the case. Change of mind must be sought out. It must be a conscious choice of us reevaluating the reality of what we think and why we think it.

Here lies the problem. Most people never do this. They never give the benefit of the doubt to anyone or anything. They just make up their mind based upon the whatever that is in their mind and then the doors for new realizations are shut. Though we can all agree this is a very low level of human consciousness, think about it, isn't this what we encounter every day? From this, as there is no new realizations allowed into the mind of most people, they never even ponder if what they are thinking is wrong. The fact is, most people don't want to admit when they are wrong because in their mind they are right.

This leaves us with a bit of a dilemma as we pass through life. Most people believe what they believe. Thus, they say what they say based upon that belief. But, that belief is not based in fact it is simply based upon belief but belief is never fact.

What do you believe? What do you say based upon your belief? What have you said based upon your belief? Have you ever taken the time to reanalyze your belief? Have you ever taken the time to actually view things from a new perspective? Have you ever recanted what you have stated based upon what you once believed? Do you possess the ability to admit that you were wrong or what you said was simply based upon a predetermined opinion that you conjured up and formulated in your own mind?

Most people are stubborn. They are stubborn in what they believe. From this they allow their ego to guide their actions in getting other people to hear and hopefully embrace what they believe. In doing this they open an entirely new realm of reality, however, as what they are doing is affecting the life, the livelihood, and the actuality of other people. By doing this, by holding fast to their projected opinion, they are causing the lives of other people to be affected and to be change. Do you have that right? Does anyone have that right? Do you or anybody else hold the right to affect the ultimately destiny of any person or anything simply because someone wishes to make up their mind and speak their mind?

What do you believe? Why do you believe it? Do you believe you have the duty or the right to influence the mind's of others by broadcasting what you believe? If you do, you are taking on a whole lot of responsibility that will ultimately affect you as your pass through your life because what you have said, based upon the temporariness of what you believe, has affected the life of someone or something else.

Think before you speak. Think about the consequence of what you speak. Be strong enough to continually reevaluate your beliefs. Admit when you are wrong.

Guardian Angels and Why They Do What They Do
22/May/2020 09:29 AM

There have been a lot of fantasy novels, TV shows, and movies that invoke the images of guardian angels. It is not uncommon for the guardian angel to be one of the parents of the person they are watching over in these depictions. Whether or not you believe in guardian angels or not is almost unimportant for that is all personal mind stuff. But, what is, more or less, important is the fact that parents would be the ones watching over the child from the ethereal realm.

Particularly in cinematic depictions, the guardian angel parent is always looking over their child after their child has gone through some life crisis or had the realization about how their parents had sent them down a dark pathway to encounter life. But, where did the instigation for that life dilemma begin? Almost universally it was caused by the parents and the way they raised that child. What they put that child through during their childhood caused that child to live their life in a specific manner.

Certainly, there is something embedded in all of us where we see our parents as some sort of savior who can help us in our time of need. But, for many of us, that was not the case even though some people hold onto that fantasy.

As I have passed through my life I have known a few people who had very supportive parents and good childhoods. But, more often than not, I have encountered people who grew up under less than ideal circumstances and from that their life was defined. Some of these people stayed in contact with their parents. Whether this is out of cultural programming or simply the belief that is the way that life is suppose to be lived, while others stepped away from contact. In either case, that did not change the damage that was done at the hands of their parents and the childhoods these people were forced to live due to the choices and the behavior of their parents.

For example, there is one person I have known for much of life. He was born to a very young mother and an older alcoholic father. The mother eventually left the father and as she was still young she would meet new men and get into relationships with them hoping to find the long-term, sought-after relationship that is promised in all the romance novels. I would witness the pain in my friend's being as each new man would come and go. This lead him to express a lot of anger in his his later years in his relationships which goes on to this day. I too encountered a lot of early life problems due to my parents doing a very poor job and making some very bad choices with rearing me. Was it my friend's fault? No. He was forced into a lifestyle and a pattern of behavior. Was it my fault? No. I, like everyone else, was created by my parents and the childhood that they provided.

Throughout my years I have known a lot of people and the ones who exhibited bad behavior were most commonly the people who had experienced what may be defined as a bad childhood. Think about it, how many people (including yourself) can you say were lead through a bad childhood via the parent's choices? How many people (including yourself) reacted to and did unsavory things in life due to the things that were done to them during their childhood?

As everyone's childhood lays the foundations for what they are to become as an adult, each person, if they take the time and truly study themselves can point to the factors that came to cause them to behave the way they behave and has caused them to do the things they do as they pass through adulthood. This is why so many people who experienced bad or abusive childhoods react the same way when they become parents.

So, what can be done about all of this? In many ways, that is one of the ultimate questions in life. Because we are all formed by our childhoods. We are all molded by what experiences we had and how our parents treated us during our childhood. The problem is, if a person does not possess the ability to truly explore themselves, and why they behave in the manner that they behave, they are simply destine to live a life dominated by what was done to them and how they were indoctrinated into life. Thus, the choice must be made by each person to very consciously attempt to form their own patterns of thought and behavior. Though this is not easy, especially if one was programmed into life by the poor choices and actions of their parents, if one does not do this they can never truly claim to be their own person. For if they don't do this then all they are is the rebroadcasted echoes of their parents and their parent's behavior.

It is not uncommon for people to look away from themselves for some spiritual intervention. Some look to guardian angels. Some cultures teach that the parents and the ancestors of a person look over them. But, let's face facts; do you want the person who guided you down a pathway that hurt your overall life evolution towards greater goodness to be the one pulling your puppet strings from the great beyond? Isn't it better that you decide to take control over your own existence, battle through any life obstacles you may encounter, and consciously make yourself the best person that you can be overcoming any of the negative programming that was introduced into you by someone who was not consciously in control of themselves and did not possess the true ability to put their child's wellbeing over their own feelings and desires?

You can believe in guardian angels if you want to. You can release the control over you life if you desire. But, if you give your powers away, just as in your childhood, you are allowing someone else to control your destiny. Is that what you really want?

What's On Your Mind?
21/May/2020 09:19 AM

Once upon a time, in the long ago and the far-far away, you had to ask someone, *"What's on your mind?"* Or, maybe a friend would call you up because they wanted to tell you something or maybe they would invite you out to lunch because they had something they needed to talk to you about. That was then, this is now. ...Now, everyone tells everybody everything. I mean, think about it, everybody puts everything out there on twitter, on Facebook, on their podcasts, on their blogs; telling all these things—expressing all these emotions to people they do not even know.

Think about your Facebook feed. Maybe you're Facebook friends with someone. But, more than likely, that someone is somebody you have never actually met. At best, maybe you've exchanged a few messages. But, there you are reading their deepest emotions put out there for the world to see.

I guess in some ways that's therapeutic. I mean, it is always taught that you need to release your emotions and don't keep them bottled up inside.

I believe that most of us have read about a person's hard breakup or health crisis. Sometimes you really feel for these people. ...People you do not even know.

Of course, there's a lot of all the other bullshit being put out there, as well. People expressing what they think about whatever it is they are thinking about. Some people love what someone says while others get pissed off. Some people just love to react. Some people try to get other people to react. Some people relish in their the ability to make other people react. They love to stir the pot. It gets them high. But, all that is just stupid.

All these people, creating all these feelings, with one thing in mind. That one thing is what is on their mind. And, that's the key to this puzzle. What they are expressing is what is on their mind. It may be also what they are living but it is essential to note, what they are doing, what they are feeling, what they are living through is not what you are living through. They have their life and you have yours. And, no matter how much anyone attempts to draw you into what they are thinking and feeling that is not what you are living. You are living what you are living and how much does that person who is attempting to draw you into their melodrama truly care about what is going on in your life?

People are a selfish breed. They do what they do based upon themselves, not upon you. That is why they are expressing what they are thinking and feeling to the unknown masses. They want the energy surge of people feeling for them even if those people do not even know who they truly are.

It's important to keep this in mind as you are forced to experience the experiences of others, because even if you can understand what someone else is going through, they are living their life just as you are living yours. What they did to get themselves to a specific juncture in their life is what they did: it was their choices, it is their karma, it is not yours. This is the same for you. You did what you did to get yourself to where you are. No matter how much you express your feelings about where you are to the all and the everyone, and no matter how much sympathy you may receive, those people are not living your destiny. They cannot. It is only you who must experience your life.

So, feel what you are feeling. You can tell it to everyone if you want to. View what others are feeling. Sympathize with them if you want to. But know that your reality is no one else's reality, just as no one else's reality is yours. Only you can live your own life. Only you can truly feel what you are feeling.

Dealing with the Powers That Be
and Playing in Your Own Playground
20/May/2020 09:44 AM

There are two distinct levels of people. There are the people who like to play by the rules and then there are those who want to break the rules—those who feel the rules don't apply to them. Of course, as one passes through life these perceptions alter and change but at the heart of any individual, at any given time in their life, they are following one of those two primary pathways.

Generally, once a person has passed from childhood into adolescence, the path they will follow takes shape. Many in their young life choose the pathway of rebellion—they feel they are above or beyond the law. There is the great scene in the movie, Rebel Without a Cause where Marlon Brando's character is asked, *"What are you rebelling against?" His answer, "What'a you got?"* And, this is the case for many young people as they chart their way into adulthood.

People are trained in the way they behave. If they are indoctrinated into structure when they are young, some attempt to follow that pathway. If, on the other hand, they grow up in a world without structure or discipline then they are more prone to follow a pathway of distaste towards authority.

For example, people who truly take the training of the martial arts to heart are commonly someone who leans towards being guided by rules, regulations, and rank structure. This is also the case of someone who decides to become part of the military. For these people, they look to the hierarchy of structure for their life definition. The problem is, in something like the martial arts, there is not a clearly defined hierarchy to the degree as say there is in the military; through it is claimed that there is. Periodically, I see long-trained practitioners becoming disenchanted with the powers-that-be of any organization because those powers are not following the promised rules.

To go deeper into this, we can look to a subject that I have discussed a few times in writings and several times during lectures. For me, someone who has been directly involved with the Korean martial arts for virtually my entire life, I have seen these martial arts, and their organizations, evolve for over fifty years. Some of the things I have witnessed during this time period would shock many and, in fact, the true-hearted practitioner would not even believe. But, I was there, I witnessed it. From my own experiences I learned to never let myself be too drawn into the promised illusion of these martial art organizations. Add into this the disintegrative mindset of some western practitioners who have risen up through the ranks and claimed control and in some cases these systems have become an in-fighting mess.

The problem is, for the most part, the traditional martial arts are based upon advancement through rank. Thus, someone must be certified by someone or some organization. Add into this the fact that many a martial artist bases their entire existence upon the insecurity based mindset of attacking others to make themselves appear to be something more than they actually are and you have all kinds of people attacking the credibility or the abilities of others. Thus, people turn to organization for their validity. But, there is a big problem in all of this.

In regard to the Korean martial arts and Korean martial arts organizations, like I have long said, and I have explained to many a western practitioner, if you do not have a South Korean, "Master," walking you through the door each time you knock, it is very common that the door will not be answered at all. Even for someone like me, with a good command of the Korean language, many times my questions have not been addressed.

This goes to the whole structure of Korean and Asian society in general. These indigenous groups tend to be very ethnocentric. Sure, if you get to be friends with a Korean born instructor in your home country or in South Korea you may have a bit of a different experience. But again, that is someone walking you through the door.

My whole life is made up of Koreans. My earliest exposure to the martial arts was from a Korean. My first martial art business was in association with a Korean. My entire extended family is Korean. So, believe me when I tell you, I know the inside of Korean culture. And, you cannot use a western mindset to define Korean culture. This is the mistake that many people make and the reason why some become disenchanted with Korean and other Asian based martial art organizations.

Early on in the modern martial arts a student was simply certified by his instructor. Like I have long said, I believe that is the best-case judgment of a student. But, times changed and large organization came to be the driving force. But, in all of that something is lost. What is lost is the true knowledge, the true relationship between the individual student and the instructor.

For the most part, the large organizations have no idea who the student's they are certifying even are. They are just a number on a certificate. But, an instructor knows that student. That is the only person who truly understands the level of advancement the student actually possesses.

But, think about this… If you removed the perpetuated illusion of rank from the martial arts, what would anyone have to prove? With no need for certification there would be no need for organizations who authorize that certification. Thus, the martial arts would then be practiced as they were truly designed, solely as a method for the physical and mental betterment of the practitioner and not as a means of ego gratification by exhibiting the rank someone has supposedly achieved.

I imagine that many of you who read this blog don't really care about the martial arts, martial art organizations, or the trials and tribulations of the individual martial arts practitioner. Okay, so how does this issue affect your life?

Few people can claim to be whole onto themselves. They need relationships. They desire family. From this, comes a combining of the individual mind into the greater mind.

What brings people together? A similar mindset.

As stated in the beginning of this piece, some people seek structure while others seek rebellion. In either case, it is one person seeking one thing. It is one person feeling a certain way and from that they seek others of a similar mind. From this grouping people take on and sometimes attack those who think a different way. Right or wrong does not matter because who is ultimately right and who is ultimately wrong? It's all a point of view.

As you pass through life you will be seeking out those of a similar mind. As you establish friendships you will create a group of those with a like mind. This group may be small or it may be large but within this group there will always be a hierarchy and thus a rank structure. Some will find solace in this group. Some will stay within the boundaries of this group forever. Others will become frustrated that their needs are not being met, they will become disillusioned, and they will leave. The thing is, as long as you are part of any group there are other people's minds, other people's needs, and other people's desires at play. In any group you can never be wholly you. No group can answer all of your needs.

So, if you find yourself disillusioned with any group you have become a part of, realize the truth. A group will never give you all you hoped for because a group is a combination of minds and a combination of minds is just that. It will never provide you with everything you need, because you are not the only one that matters to a group. At best, you are simply another member of the group, just another clog in the wheel. You can be replaced.

Put your faith in people: one on one. Not in organizations.

Who Wrote What and Why
19/May/2020 10:44 AM

Every now and then I am confronted with the reality that someone has taken some of my written research and either just absconded with it outright or turned a few words around and used it as their own. I get it, in this day and age of the internet anything goes and no one cares about anyone else. Why should they? People can pretty much get away with anything; copyright infringement or not.

But, in many ways, it all goes deeper than that. There is the truth and the reality of publication that we all hope to believe. We want to believe what people are saying, particularly if it is written. It's just natural. It's the way we have all been brought up. If it's on the page, it must be real. But, the fact of reality is, so often it is not.

This is particularly the case with certain authors. Sure, some people site references on what they present. But, what is the sourcepoint of that reference?

I think back to this one editor and so-called author I used to work with. …I detailed a much more uncompromising depiction of the falling apart of our relationship several years ago in this blog when the guy became a total asshole after I saved his ass with an article I composed that his magazine could not have gone to publication without. But anyway, that was then…

As a magazine editor, this guy had a line to large publishing houses. From this, he had several books published all based upon martial arts facts and history. The problem was, he did not write his own words. He got people like me to write his chapters for him. As the man never went to college, he did not understand the protocols of publishing where someone who is doing that takes, *"Editor,"* credit not, *"Author,"* credit. But, that is exactly what he did. He always listed himself as the sole author. Thus, people like myself, who actually wrote his books for him, would never get paid a dime and, at best, receive a, *"Thanks."*

Today, I came upon a site that used a couple of this man's books as the reference for the martial art history section on the website. He listed the aforementioned editor as the author. But, as stated, though this guy claimed authorship, I provided all of the Korean martial art research in his books, which is what this site focused upon. ...I so remember the day this man contacted me and asked me about putting that research together for him for this one specific book that was referenced. As I had already complied years and years of research into the Korean martial arts, I sent it over to him later that afternoon and he was just blown away, thanking me so much. Did I get author credit? Nope... Yet, I did all the work.

I think in many ways a lot of people can relate to these goings-on. Think about all of the people who work for companies; they toil day in and day out and they struggle to make ends meet. They do this while the bosses and the owner make big money and live really well. They live a great lifestyle all provided by the labor of others. Certainly, not right but that is the way it is. In fact, it is the way it has seemingly always been.

You know, this is the problem with life... We all must work to survive. We all must develop relationships that we hope will lead us to something better. We all try to try. But, more often than not, we are held back by the actions of others—we never get the credit or the thanks that we deserve. We certainly, never get paid what we are worth. So, we are left with someone else being allowed to take credit and gain from our labor.

This is not the first time I have been confronted with this fact. But, the reality is, even if I were to tell the person who runs the website that I was the one who actually did the research and wrote the words that are presented in that guy's book, why should he believe me? The other guy's name is on the cover.

Now, I could go into the whole thing about karma here and all that. But, who cares? Did the guy who took credit for my research and my writings care when he took authorship of those books? Nope… He took the money and he took the ego gratifications and he never looked back. For everyone who knows nothing else, he was the author. Today, he still is the author, even though he has since passed away.

I am sure there is something that we can all learn from this but I am not quite sure what it is. We all do what we can to survive. We all do what we can to get over. We all do what we can to make our life and the life of those we care about better. We do this, but more often than not the price we pay is hardly worth what we receive as all anyone else does is to take credit for our caring enough to do and then they either trash or forget our names in the process.

Welcome to life.

*   *   *

19/May/2020 07:15 AM

For each of us we have dreams that we really don't like. But, no matter how horrendous the dream we know that sooner or later we are going to wake up.

What about life? What about when you are living through a terrible life event or living a life that you really don't like? How do you wake up from that?

When Bad Things Happen
18/May/2020 07:46 AM

A lot of people do a lot of bad things to people. Do they care about the damage they are causing to the life of the person whom they are hurting? No, or they would not be doing what they are doing.

A lot of people do a lot of good things to people. Do they care about the goodness, help, and the care that they are unleashing? Probably, but because they are doing what they are doing from the perspective of goodness that is not their true motivation, they just want to help.

A lot of people do a lot of bad things. Think about how many movies, TV shows, novels, or song lyrics are based upon the bad actions of some person doing some bad thing. Think about your life, think about some of the people you have known, have any of us passed through life without something bad happening to us—something bad that was instigated and done to us by somebody else? Probably not. And, some of those things that happened were very-very bad. They changed our life forever.

Did the person who did them think or care about how much hurt they were unleashing onto our life? Most likely, no. They did what they did and they did it based upon some self-motivated something and that self-motivated something had nothing to do with helping the life of anyone else but themselves.

Some people create damage with a smile upon their face. They do what they do and they take pride in it. Some people create damage and they do it from a, whoa is me perspective. "Look how poor and pathetic I am. Look what the world has done to me. Look what some person has done to me." From this, they justify their hurting action(s) onto the life of someone else.

No matter what the motivation, no matter what the explanation, no matter what the justification, when someone hurts someone else, that someone who has been hurt is never really the same. In fact, sometimes their life is left damaged or destroyed forever. If nothing else, it is left changed forever. How much does the instigator of that action care? Very little, if at all, because if they cared about the feelings and the life of anyone else they would not have done the hurtful action they unleashed in the first place. Yet, many of these hurtful people relish in the power they feel by taking from or hurting others, they relish in the possession they have gained by stealing, and they relish in the experiences they have gaining by doing their hurtful actions.

Most of us have felt hurt, brought on by someone else, to one degree or another. Some of those hurts are life defining. They hurt forever. This is especially the case when what someone has done is not undone.

Some things can't be undone. Other things can. But, how often does the person who has done the hurtful action cared enough about the pain they have caused anyone else to do anything to undo the hurt they have unleashed? Thus, many a person's life is left damaged forever.

Some hurtful actions are small. Recently, someone stole my 1957 Fender Tweed Deluxe Amp out of my car. Why did they take it? Did they even know what it was? Did they target me to hurt me? I don't know? All I know is that I had it forever, I really loved it, I created some great music with it, and now it is gone.

Some would say that is a small hurt, and I would agree. But, it does hurt. Something I cared about was stolen from me and the person who took it may be happy they hurt someone else, they may not care that they hurt someone else, or they may have just done it for the money they will receive by selling it. I doubt that they stole it to create music.

In this same vein, I remember back in the '80. I had literally just bought this new Jeep. The same day I purchased it I parked it in front of my apartment in Hermosa Beach. I went in for maybe fifteen minutes and by the time I came out someone had stolen the radio that was in it. Brand new car, no radio, all in just a couple of minutes. I was so upset. Again, some would say that's a small thing and I would agree; yet small things can turn into big things and small things can come to define a life because every action leads to a reaction and if the instigation for any action is based upon negativity there can only be one ultimate result. The people who steal rarely care about the person they are stealing from. Some even hope to take so that they can hurt the life of that person. But, more than all that, hurt can be unleashed on so many levels and it can do so much damage to the life of the person that is being hurt. The damage can hurt at the moment but the pain may last for a lifetime. But, if the person who does the hurting does not care about the hurt that they unleash, if they are proud or empowered by what they have done, what does this tell us about humanity? We all can see what it tells us about that bad-thing inducing person, but what about the bigger picture? Why are people allowed to do bad things?

Ultimately, I doubt that there is any answer for this. And, I doubt that there is anyone out there who cannot point to some pain, some hurt, or some stealing that has been done to their life. Did that hurt come to define your existence? Did it cause you too to do bad things to other people? Or, did it motivate you to become a better person and only do good, helpful things?

For some, life is easy. For others, they have encountered pain brought on by someone else and in some cases this has come to be a life defining pain. What can we do? What can you do? The answer: hurt no one, take from no one. Care about everyone. Do everything you can to undo any pain you have caused. And, never allow the hurt, the pain, or the bad things that have been done to you to become the definition of your life.

And, oh yeah, if anyone out there has a '57 Fender Tweed Deluxe Amp or something similar they want to turn me onto, let me know.

Undo the hurt!

The Definitions in Your Mind
17/May/2020 08:09 AM

Who am I to you? How do you define me? Am I an author, a filmmaker, a musician, an artist, a martial artists, a philosopher or am I simply an asshole who has written too many words on too many pages, a guy who has made too many weird movies, a man who has created too much music that you don't want to listen to, or someone who has painted a bunch of paintings that you don't really like?

Here's the thing, however you define me, is that me or is that simply how you have defined me in your mind? Is your definition of me valid simply because you believe it to be so or is it simply your interpretation of me based upon however it is you feel about whatever it is you are feeling?

How about how people have defined you? Think about a definition that someone assigned to you at some point in your life. Was that a valid definition? Was the definition a true portrayal of you or was simply how they intrepid you to be and whether or not they like what you do?

For most people, if they think to the way other people have defined them, they quickly realize that the definitions that others have assigned to them are wholly or at least in part incorrect. Though they realize this about themselves and the definitions that others have assigned to them, they continue to do it to other people—they continue to cast definitions to the life of others.

How about you? Think out to the people that you think about. What definition do you place upon them? Do you ever consider the fact that the definition you assign is simply that—something you have concocted in your own mind? Do you ever consciously realize that what you think about them is nothing more than what you think about them and because it is you interpreting them and their life actions that more than likely they see themselves and what they do in an entirely different way than you do?

Do you tell people what you think about other people? Do you discuss with people your interpretations of the life and the doings of other people? Do you tell people your definition of someone else? Have you ever been wrong? Have you ever changed your mind about someone? If so, what does that tell you about the definitions that you hold? It should tell you that definitions are temporal—that your definitions are defined by your own limited understanding about an individual. It should explain that they change as you change. Knowing this, why do you cast your judgments in the first place?

Have the definitions that someone else expressed about you ever damaged your life? Have the definitions you expressed about someone else ever damaged their life?

It is easy to define a person out there in the distance. It is easy to cast your judgment on someone you do not know. But, if you do this, if you cast your judgments onto others, all you have done is to express your limited life perception because if you do not know a person, on a personal level, how can you truly know anything about them at all?

Even when you personally know a person, do you truly know them? Many people put out a persona to the world. They express an image of how they wish to be perceived. Though that persona is how they wish to be viewed, in many cases, if a person is not a consciously true representation of themselves, then all they are is the illusion they are presenting. In other words, people lie about who and what they truly are.

People also change. They change for the better and they change for the worse. Many things can bring about change in a person but change causes change—change makes the person you once knew into an entirely new and different being. From this, the person you once knew and how you defined them may have changed. They may have become a different person. Then what?

What happens to your definition?

The main thing to understand about life is that unless you truly know a person, you can never even come close to knowing them. Even if you think you do know them, who they are may simply be a projected illusion or a flat out lie. Or, they may change.

What can we conclude from all of this? We can conclude that it is only the self-unaware that believe that they know anyone. It is only the egotistical and the arrogant that attempt to project their definitions onto other people. For the truth of the life is, you cannot define anyone because you are not them, and without being them, at best, you only possess a very limited understanding of their reality.

Work on yourself and stop placing your definitions onto the life of other people because more often than not, your definition is wrong.

*　　*　　*

16/May/2020 12:40 PM

Your life is based upon the foundations that were laid out for you and the foundations of the choices you have made.

What are the foundations of your life?

*   *   *
15/May/2020 04:19 PM

If you record a silent song can it be considered music?

Most People Don't Give Back
15/May/2020 09:17 AM

Right now, today, what are your plans for giving anything to anybody? When you woke up this morning did you have a game plan in place for what you were going to do for someone today? Yesterday, what did you do for someone? The day before that, what did you do for anybody?

Most people are very centered on themselves. They think about themselves and maybe those people they care about. They think about what they want, how they are feeling, and how people are reacting to them, but they spend very little of their Life Time turning off Self Thought and actually doing something for someone else.

Think about it, who have you helped lately? Who did you think about, who did you decide needed some help, and who did you actually provide that help to?

If you did provide help, how did that helping help you? Was your helping actually given from a pure perspective of caring or was your giving motivated by what you would receive?

Think about your life... Think about your Right Now... What plan do you have to help anyone? Are you planning to help anyone?

Sure, you may be having all kinds of problems in your life. Sure, you may be very busy. Sure, you may be working hard to make ends meet. All of these are common excuses. But, excuses are just excuses. They arise from a very self-centered perspective.

All of those excuses, being as they are, who are you going to help? Who are you planning to give to? What are you planning to do for anyone but yourself?

There are a lot of people who need help out there. What are you going to do about it?

Sure, helping can be big. It can be giving someone some money; buying them something that they need. It can be giving them a place to stay when they have no roof over their head. It can be giving them a job. It can be helping them move. It can be buying them a meal. Or, it can be holding their hand when their heart is broken. Helping can also be small. It can be saying a nice word when someone else is saying something negative. It can be smiling at a person. It can be telling something that you appreciate that they exist, that you are happy that they are in your life. Helping can be anything but to help, "Helping," has to be actualized. It has to be you stepping outside of your Self Involvement and actually doing something for someone else.

Try it, help someone, and watch everything become just a little bit better.

* * *

15/May/2020 09:16 AM

If you've hurt somebody and you think that's okay, you should really think again.

*   *   *

15/May/2020 09:16 AM

If you don't want something to be true but it is true does that make it a lie?

*   *   *

14/May/2020 10:41 AM

Not every picture you take is going to be in focus.

* * *

14/May/2020 10:17 AM

A teacher can provide you with the fundamentals but it is the student who must decide if they are going to practice hard enough to master the techniques.

What Part You Play in What You Play
14/May/2020 09:09 AM

I was kicking around eBay and I noticed this very rare book written by my teacher, Swami Satchidananda. Once upon a time I had a copy of that book, back when it first came out in '78, but through time, giving things away to other people, and the whatever, I have not owned a copy of it for a couple of decades. Seeing it, and being reminded of it, of course I purchased it. But, that's not the story…

…The story is, this book is made up of lectures given by Swami Satchidananda. On the copyright page they list the names of the people who helped bring the book to publication. Meaning, the people who donated money to get the book printed. The one person they do not have listed is me. Me, the person who recorded all of the lectures that make up the words that are in that book.

As is well documented, I was Swami Satchidananda's soundman for a number of years. I was the one who recorded his lectures for posterity. Once they were recorded, I turned the tapes over to the powers that be. I never charged a dime for any of my services: for the sound equipment, the set up, the tape decks, the tapes, the travel, or my lodging, I was happy to do it. It was karma yoga. And, the thing is, which some people may not realize, if it wasn't me doing it, I don't know who would have done it. They would have had to hire an outside source and pay them big bank.

I really tried hard to do a good job doing the sound for Gurudev. Whether it was a small crowd of a hundred or a gigantic lecture of a thousand or more, I gave it my all. I tried to make the sound perfect and I recorded everything on reel-to-reel and cassette. But, the thing is, though I viewed the recordings as an art form, it was not like I would sign the tapes with my name like say an artist would do on a painting. So, once I handed them off, as they were passed down the line, no one knew what I had done. From this, my name is not in the, *"Thanks,"* category of the book.

Did it bother me back then? I don't know, maybe? Does it bother me now? Probably a bit more.

As it was karma yoga, I get it… I did it as a means of selfless service. So, no payment required. But, I am sure the people who tossed in some money to get the book published believed they were doing karma yoga, as well. Yet, their name got mentioned. But, the fact is, that book would not be in existence if it were not for me. So???

Life is a complicated process. Everybody is doing something. Most people spend their time, wasting their time, however. Few people create anything. For me, it is always the creator/the artist who walks the highest level of humanity. Whether that art is painting, writing, making movies, creating music, giving lectures to help people become the best version of themselves that they can be, or recording those lectures so they are cast to the annals of time, art is the highest good. But sometimes, no matter how much the artist sees what they are doing as art, the artist's name is forgotten; it is left out of the screen credits. The answer, I don't know… I guess you just have to know it was you and you gave something to the something of reality even if the world forgets your name.

Reinventing Yourself
12/May/2020 09:39 AM

Do you ever think about reinventing yourself? Do you ever think about changing who you are? Do you ever ponder doing things differently than the way you always do them?

Most people fall into a pattern fairly early in their late adolescence and/or early adult life. They begin to do things the way they do them and they change very little as they pass through their life. Yes, some people alter a few of their traits here or there but on the whole most people maintain being who they are throughout their life.

Many people, as they become older, find that they are dissatisfied with their life. Perhaps they did not achieve all of the things that they had hoped to achieve when they were younger. Most young people see the future as promising. Though they may not have what they want today, they believe they will achieve it tomorrow. The problem is, for the majority of the world's people, this is not the case. That achievement never happens. From this, many are left dissatisfied with their life.

There is the others side of this, as well, the person who has accomplished some, many, or all of their goals. As they are doing pretty much what they want to do and are receiving the desired admiration from their friends, family, and colleagues, they are fairly content with who and what they are, how they are doing what they are doing, and where they find themselves in life. Why should they reevaluate their life?

There are many motivations as to why a person would reevaluate and change their life. Most people never take the time to truly review where they find themselves in life, however. They make excuses for where they are and what they are doing. But, an excuse is only that, it is just an excuse.

Every now and then you will find someone who takes the bull by the horns and changes. They make a conscious decision and they redirect their life. They change their trajectory. These people are inspirational. Whether this redirected life change is a major alteration in their career or in the way they emotionally encounter and interact with other people, their change can be an inspiration to us all.

So, here's the question… Who should change their life? Who should reinvent themselves?

Reinvention must be a personal choice and/or realization. For no one can tell you to do anything. If you change for someone else or because someone tells you that you need to change, that change usually is packaged with a lot of resentment and, due to this fact, it rarely lasts.

But, again, who should change their life?

Ask yourself, how do you feel about you? How do you feel about where you are in life? How do you feel about the way in which you interact with others? How do you feel about what you are giving back to the world?

These are tricky questions because of the fact that the successful person may immediately believe that everything with their life is fine. But, is it? If you are successful, are you whole, honest, giving, and complete with yourself? Or, are you simply basing your self-decided okay-ness on the egotistical fact that you are the center of attention?

For the person who finds themselves unfulfilled or unhappy in life, the answer to the questions comes much more easily. *"I want more." "I want to feel better." "I want to be happy."* Okay, what are you going to do about it?

To be a True Person, to be true to yourself, you need to be brutally honest with yourself. You need to define your placement in this reality. You need to not only see yourself as you see yourself but you need to see yourself as others see you. You need to look at what you truly are and what you are truly giving to the life of other people.

If you want to change, if you feel you need to change, this is the time to change. Set out on a course. First decide that you want to change. Design a pathway, a game plan for your change. Then, make yourself follow that pathway no matter what. Because it is only you who can truly orchestrate any reinvention of yourself and if you do not try wholeheartedly then there is only you to blame.

Your life is defined by what you feel. Your life is defined by what you do. Your life is defined by how others see you. Your life is defined by how you react to others. Your life is defined by how others react to you.

Everything begins with you. Who are you? What are you? What are you doing to become the best you that you can be? If you are doing nothing, you are doing nothing.

If you want to change, if you want to make you a better you, if you want to become the you that you always wanted to be become, begin to do it right now. Decide to change. Decide to become. Design a pathway and reinvent yourself. Stop wasting your Life Time.

Listen for the Subtleties
11/May/2020 04:26 PM

When you are listening to music do you listen for the subtitles? Do you listen for the variances of tone, pitch, tempo, note structure, and oscillation? Do you listen for the subtle alterations in the texture of the music?

Most people when they are listening to music either like it or they don't. They enjoy listening to music where they like the beat or the voice of the singer; maybe they like the lyrics. But, how many people—do you, attempt to identify the subtle nature that is taking place within any composition that you are listening to?

The fact is, a lot of music is very basis. It is a singer finding a style of music that they like and fits their lyrics. Like the listener, they don't think about the subtleties of the sound too much either. But, if you don't listen for the subtitles in the sound so much of the heart and the essence of music is lost.

There are a lot of true composers and musicians out there. They truly delve into the art of music creation. Not only do they do that on the level of composition but they also do that when they are recording and onto mixing the songs once they have been recorded. They are truly focusing on presenting a unique presentation of their musical creation.

It is easy to say, *"I like,"* or, *"I don't like,"* a piece of music. But, that is almost animalistic. That takes no art. That takes no developed understanding. That's just self-motivated judgment. But, if you can step beyond the mind, there is an entirely new realm of understanding that can be found and embraced by listening to and studying the subtleties that exist within a musical creation.

Many people simply use music as a means to block out the sounds of the world. They have music playing in the earbuds all the time. They do this so much so that they are no longer listening to the music. It is there but they are just thinking about something else. Again, with this practice, the true greatest of music appreciation is lost.

Try this, next time you are listening to music, take the time, silence your mind, and really hear what you are listening to. Seek out and find the subtleties in the creation. Isolate them. Identify them. With this, not only do you increase your deepening knowledge of music but you can also come to appreciate the true artistic focus of the composer, the musician, and the engineers, as well.

Truly listen and all of life becomes more refined.

* * *

11/May/2020 04:24 PM

If you define your life upon the accolades or the awards presented to you by someone else you never will truly wholly be yourself because your entire life becomes defined by what someone else thinks of you.

* * *

11/May/2020 09:21 AM

How much would you pay to know the secret of the universe?

The Something That You Did Not Say
10/May/2020 08:39 AM

I believe that most of us have encountered one of those situations where we were talking to someone about something and the conversation ended. Maybe it was an hour, a day, a week, a month, or even a year later when we realized that we did not tell that someone we were having that conversation with that some essentially important something that had to do with that conversation. We forget to state a fact or to put in the caveat that would have changed the other person's complete understanding about what was being discussed. We met, we talked, we ended the conversation, we left, but then we realized we forgot to tell that person that some important something.

In some cases, we can recontact the individual and pick up the conversation where we left off. But, this is not always the case. Sometimes, when a conversation is over it is over. And, that conversation, what was said and all that other person heard, is all that they have to base their whatever upon. Then what?

Conversations are the key form of communications in life. In conversations you get to express what you think, what you feel, what you believe; you get to explain the you that is you. That is why it is such an essential element in life.

I believe we have all had the experience when we are communicating with someone we say something and it, *"Came out wrong."* It came out in a way we really didn't mean. Or, what was said was interpreted in a manner that was not intended. Of course, this style of discourse has the possibly of causing all kinds of discord but, if a person is open and understanding, what was said and misconstrued can be recommunicated.

But, what about when what was said was what was said and that's all you get? You know/you realize that you should have said something else but you cannot?

One of the key fundamentals of life (and some would say

key problems of life) is that people create their definition of a person by their conversations. If their conversation(s) with another individual is limited to one or two times then a complete misunderstanding about the things that have taken place with that other person or what that others person's interpretation of reality and life events are can be completely misunderstood.

We all think, we all feel, we all live our life, we all attempt to portray our life experiences and our life feelings to other people. But, there are times when we forget to explain that one key something that will change the entire dynamic of understanding in the mind of some other person.

Just like a jigsaw puzzle that is missing one of its pieces, without a completely presentation of all of one's life components, true and complete understanding can never be gained. Moreover, if someone has altered the structure of the puzzle, i.e. with a lie, complete understanding can never be gained.

So, think about this, how many times has anyone ever had a complete understanding of your all and your everything? How many times has someone known the all and the everything about your whatever? How many times has anyone been presented with the complete understanding of your reality to the degree that they actually think what you think and feel what you feel? The true answer is probably never.

It is important to take in consideration, as no one ever truly understands the knowledge that you have, the feelings that you feel, and the truth that is you, it is doubtful that even if you had added that one caveat to the conversation they would still probably not completely understand the reality that you have lived and the emotions that you have felt.

What does this tell us? It tells us, sure, try to convey what you have lived and what you are feeling to others, but if you miss a point here or there, don't worry about it, because the reality of the reality is, few people are going to care enough about you to truly be able to step beyond their own desire-based melodrama to actually understand or care about the you that is truly you anyway.

The Media Lies
09/May/2020 01:47 PM

There is this group of antique stores I like to go to in Orange County. I was watching the news last night and they were discussing how some of the Stay at Home Suggestions are finally being lifted here in California during this COVID-19 Coronavirus Pandemic. Hand-in-hand with this, some businesses are being allowed to open.

In the newscast's presentation, they showed footage from these antique stores. Though I though that it was a bit strange, as these antique stores are far from essential businesses, I pondered that Orange County does have a bit of a different approach to life than does say, L.A. County. So, what the heck, I hopped in my car this morning, and after not having driven on the freeways for over two months, took the thirty-five mile or so drive, and went down to O.C planning to do some antiquing. Arriving, I witnessed that all of the stores that they showed footage from on the newscast are still closed. The news had lied to me.

We all hope to believe the news. Isn't that the basis for much of our decision-making? But, think about it, how often does the media create their stories to present their own interpretation of the news. For example, when the Trump Administration has an accomplishment or makes some sort of headway, news services like Fox News and other right leading media outlets, praise it. Whereas networks like CNN or MSNBC find a reason to find fault in it. Did the facts change? No, not at all, simply the interpretation of what happened was presented in a specific manner. This was the same during the Obama era. CNN would praise the actions whereas networks like FOX would find fault.

I've spent a fair percentage of my life outside of the U.S. and from that vantage point I have clearly seen how the interpretation of the news is slanted by the media. For example, you watch CNN International and the story will be told one way, view the local national networks and their interpretation may be very different. Did the news change? No, simply its interpretation is altered.

So, what does this tell us? It tells us that not only do people but the organizations that we place our trust into, at best, do nothing more than present their interpretation of life happenings to suit their own agenda. Is this right? No, it is not. But, it is the way it is. And, most people simply listen to so-called news the way they want to hear it presented. Thus, giving birth to the various networks that present news in a specific manner.

So, the next time you hear something on the news, be sure to see through the slanted interpretation and analyze why a particular news agency is reporting something the way they are reporting it. Be prudent in listening for and piercing through the commentary that is placed in association with any so-called fact.

And, oh yeah, don't be fooled by stock footage, call up an antique store to see if they are actually opened before you make the drive to it after seeing something on the news.

* * * 09/May/2020 07:21 AM

If you could change the station would you be watching the dream that is being broadcast on the TV screen of your mind?

Expounding What You Don't Know
08/May/2020 01:39 PM

I forever find it interesting/funny when someone points me in the direction of some long discourse about something and while reading it, though the person is making all kinds of claims about their knowledge of the subject and presenting what they think as facts, they are completely wrong. I mean, don't these people feel bad when they are telling someone something about what they know but what they think they know is factually incorrect?

I have all kinds of thoughts about why people do this kind of stuff, and I've spoken about some of them in the past, but that's not the point of the all this... The fact is, these presentations take time to produce. Whether they are written essays or video presentations, that kind of stuff takes time, focus, energy, and effort to create. Some of them are presented as a goof or a joke. That's a whole different ball game and I'm not talking about that. But, a lot of these presentations are presented as if they are factually based discourses. They reference talk-points, they provide examples, but what they never do is find out the true facts. Yet, the people who create these studies present their discourse as if it were based in facts. But, when their facts are wrong, that should make them feel a certain kind of way, but it, (apparently), does not because they never attempt to correct their mistakes.

As someone who has written for a lot of established publishers, not to mention my time in grad school, and all of the academic papers I have written or contributed to that never find their way into the mainstream media, I always had to provide factually based references for everything that I stated. But, that's all out the window now with this world of self-published everything.

Certainly, one of things I know the most about, from an

experiential standpoint, is my films. I was there. I made the movies. I know everything about them. But, time and time again I am made aware of somebody stating something as fact about these films and/or the creative process that was undertaken in their creation and what these people are stating is totally wrong. Because they are wrong, that should make the researcher feel bad that they did not correctly do their job and/or that they are presenting factually inaccurate information to the world. But, does this stop them? No. Do they ever correct their erroneous statement or conclusions? No. They just put it out there for the world to see and believe. But, they are wrong! And, wrong is never right.

What is the benefit of this? What does it help? Who does it help? What does it make better?

To belabor this fact just a little bit more, for me, (the person who was actually involved in the making of these films), I find the mistakes, the incorrect conclusions, and the lies these people tell almost funny. But, I have also witnessed the downside of all this when people have contacted me having believed what some person has falsely claimed.

This is not simply a personal thing about the films I have created. I have spent much of adult life doing cultural, demographic, and historic research. From this, there are a few subjects that I possess a large amount of factually acquired knowledge about. But, I continually see people who have never taken the time to truly do their research about what they write or speak and then putting all of this information out there simply because they heard something from someone or they concluded something simply because that is what they want to believe. This doesn't help anyone or anything. Yet, so much of what is out there and taken in by the masses is based in nothing more than someone's opinion.

Now, we all know the internet is full of tons and tons of falsities, personal biases, and flat out self-promoting lies. That being said, shouldn't the person who is creating these discourse(s) posses the level of self-respect that would cause them to present verifiable, factually accurate information instead of simply what they think about whatever they think about? Because isn't it embarrassing, or shouldn't it be embarrassing for them, if what they are presenting is wrong? But, I guess when there's no authoritative board grading on the factual accuracy of a piece, who cares?

I believe that most of the people who read this blog are aware of the fact that not everything that is seen or presented on the internet, (and other places), is real and/or factual. I also believe that most of the people who follow this blog are not the people out there doing this style of dissemination. But, it is out there everywhere and some people believe the lie. That's just not a good thing.

We all think what we think. We all have our likes and our dislikes and our opinions. We all wish things to be a certain way but, for those of us who care about the betterment of humanity, we should understand that simply because we want something to be a certain way or we interpret something to be a certain way we should not try to make it so simply because we want it to be that way. We should never present what we think as factual information because all that does is damage the all and the everything of anyone who believes it—believes it when it is not the truth.

So... Can you be more that what you think or believe? Can you care enough about the truth to not damage the truth based upon your estimation or judgment about how you wish the truth to be portrayed? Can you be more than someone who soils the life, creations, culture, or historic reality of anyone or anything by not attempting to tell people what you believe based upon nothing more than what you project the truth to be? Can you focus on you, making you a better you, instead of creating a false reality for everyone else by focusing on something that you possess no true fact-based knowledge about?

Your life is In You. Your life is not Out There. As long as you focus on the Out There, the In You can never find its way to perfection.

I Don't Have Any Hobbies
08/May/2020 10:15 AM

I was having this discussion with this lady the other day and she was taking about people and their hobbies. She asked me about my hobbies. And, though it is one of those things that I rarely consciously think about, I explained, I don't have any hobbies.

For anyone who knows me or knows about me they know that there are a lot of things that I do. A lot of things that some people would consider hobbies. But, to me, those things are me. They are my life.

For example, a lot of people see the martial arts as a hobby. But, for me, the martial arts are a lifestyle. A lot of people see painting, photography, poetry, writing, or music as a hobby, but for me, that is my livelihood. All that I do is what makes me who I am.

I think hobbies are good. I know my mother used to crochet. She would sit around for hours with a cup of coffee, her cigarette in her ash tray, and crochet. She made a lot of really good stuff. But, she did it as a distraction. She did it because she liked to do it.

That's a good example of a hobby. There are all kinds of things out there that people do simply because they like to do them and they equal nothing more than making them feel good or relaxed.

I used to have this shrink and she would ask me what do I do to relax? I didn't have an answer then and I don't have one now. I'm always on and doing. And, when I am not doing I feel very unaccomplished. I have never been one of those people who can just sit back, chill, play video games or whatever, and forget the world. In fact, I have never played a video game.

I guess I can blame my mother for she was so proud of the

fact that when she was pregnant with me she used to proudly exclaim, *"All I did was drink coffee and smoke cigarettes."* That was her generation. They didn't know about all the damage that can be done to the unborn. But, whatever the causation, as Popeye would say, *"I yam what I yam and that's all I yam."*

The reason I discus this is that we each are examples—we each become examples of what's in our minds of what is broadcast by our personality. Sure, how we got to that state can be traced via biology and defined with psychotherapy, but whatever the cause, we are what we are. We do what we do. Sure, we can change if we want to change. But, if what we are doing is functional—at least function via our own life definition and it is helpful to us and hurtful to no one, then why would we change?

The problem with many people's lives, however, is they do not define a difference between what they want out of life and what they are doing with their life. If your hobby makes you money, is it a hobby? If your hobby makes you happier or healthier, is it a hobby? But, if your hobby distracts you from making money or reaching your life goals, then that hobby has become a life actualizing hindrance.

Think how many people go through their life and get to the end of their days and feel that they have wasted their life. Think about how many make up stories or tell lies about who they are because they have not lived the life that they hoped to live. But, what kept them from that? Who kept them from achieving what they hoped to achieve? For many, the answer to that question is themselves. The reason, they existed in a world of distraction—of allowing distraction to become their life focus rather than doing something that actually equaled something.

How about you? Are you doing what you want to do that will leave your life feeling accomplished at the end of your days? Or, are you just killing time with distraction(s) as your life passes by leaving you feeling unaccomplished as you pursue your hobbies?

What you do with your life is your choice. Just be aware, what you do with your life time comes to define your life time. Hobbies are great but if they keep you from becoming all that you hope to be, then you might want to rethink what you are spending your time doing. Think about it…

* * *

08/May/2020 07:07 AM

If you are constantly telling people what you already are, you leave little room for becoming anything new.

Making It Better Is Not Making You Better
07/May/2020 10:43 AM

Many people spend much of their lives focused outside of themselves. This is particularly the case when the individual does not possess a strong sense of self-accomplishment. People focus on things outside of themselves because by doing so they do not have to focus on themselves. Though from this practice they may achieve a certain sense of accomplishment, by doing so they never become the something more that they truly hope to be.

If you explain this to someone who practices this style of life behavior, they will almost assuredly deny it. But, from their denial you can view the true nature of who they are.

Look at life… Study the people you know… How many of them are focused on self-development—becoming the best person that they can be from a physical, psychological, and spiritual perspective? How many of them truly put their ego aside and try to make themselves a better, more whole and complete representation of human life?

For most, when they look out to the psychological makeup of those around them, they will find people that are almost universally focused on things outside of themselves. This may be a sports team, a community group, the love a particular style of music, onto the discussion and the debate about what is right and wrong with cinema, politics, and society, you name it... Many of these people who focus on things outside of themselves find tools to force their ideology onto others. All across the internet you find people attempting to broadcast what they believe is right; who is right and/or who or what is wrong. Some, with a lot of time on their hands, find websites like YouTube where they make videos of themselves discussing what they believe is right or wrong or Wikipedia where they become an, "Editor," and from there, (as anyone can be an editor on Wikipedia), they go on a rampage attempt to delineate what they believe is right or wrong about whatever, anyone, or anything. But, how does that style of behavior help anything for the individual? How does it make them a better person? At best, all it does is give them a life distraction and a reason to believe that they are doing something so they do not actually have to take a look at who and what they truly are and become something more or something better on an internal level.

This is the thing about people who live their lives outside of themselves, they forever find a reason to be, *"Out there,"* they always find a justification for them doing what they do, *"Out there."* But, they never take the time to realize that as long as they are doing whatever it is they are doing, "Out there," they are not taking the time to become the better person that they can be.

How about you? Do you place your focus on the, *"Out there?"* Do you find your life distraction by existing in the, *"Out there?"* Do you attempt to broadcast your worthiness to the, *"Out there?"* Or, do you focus on the, "Inner you," becoming the best representation of who and what you can and should be?

The fact is, all the emotions are in the, *"Out there."* That is where you find love, happiness, exaltation, and anger. But, all that is just Mind Stuff. The emotion(s) you feel today will be gone tomorrow. It/they will not last. But, when you take the time to focus and train your mind to become that, "True you," that actual, *"Something more,"* it is there that you may find the true purpose of your life and actually become the best form of you as you truly give back to life.

So, what are you going to do, focus on all that temporal, meaningless stuff, *"Out there?"* Or, are you going to take the time, actually center your mind and truly take the time to become the true embodiment of something good, whole, giving, and great?

* * *

06/May/2020 01:58 PM

You can't appreciate what you don't understand.

Who You Walk Down the Road With
05/May/2020 04:14 PM

Who you walk down the road with through your life is going to define what your life will ultimately become. Who you associate with is going to help you in creating your life.

Many people lock themselves into a pattern of friendships, leading to a pattern of behavior, early in their life. From this, their entire life is defined by something that originated in their youth. Other people expand and grow their base of associations throughout their existence, adapting to where they find themselves in life. Though locking yourself into a pattern of relationships early in your life is not a bad thing, as long as those friendships guide you towards you become the best you that you can be, the opposite can also be true. Locking yourself into a pattern of behavior defined by those around you can also lead your life towards being defined by negativity and limitations if the people you associate with embrace a undesirable lifestyle.

Think about an early point in your life. Think about the person or the people you were associating with. How did those relationships come to define that time in your life? Did it help you become all that you wanted to be? Did it answer your needs? Or, did it guide you down a pathway that ultimately led you to a place that you wish you had never encountered? Did who you associated with back then cause you to become who you are today?

Now, move forward in your life. Think about a time one, five, ten, or twenty years ago where you met someone that you felt could help you gain something that you wanted out of life. How did that relationship turn out? Did it help you? Did it hurt you? Did you accomplish any of the things that you hoped you would accomplish by being in a liaison with that person? And, if you had not met them how would your life have turned out differently?

For most of us, we can point to people in our lives that have helped us to become what we have become. We can realize the people that have helped us and we can recognize the people who tried to help us. In many ways, many people forget or diminish those people who helped them in their life, however, because once they achieved what they achieve, via the help of that person, that relationship was discarded. Have you done that?

How do you think about that person who helped or tried to help you in your past? Do your ever even think about that person who aided you in gaining what you hoped to gain in life? Do you ever give them credit for what you eventually achieved? Or, do you not mention them or diminish their contribution?

Though many people that you associate with may have helped your life, there are also those who hurt your life. Think about your life, what part did you play in the evolution of your relationship with the person that helped to define your life in either a positive or a negative manner? How did you help the relationship? How did you hurt the relationship? And, what part did you play in the final definition of that relationship?

Look to someone who was in your life that is no longer in your life. …Someone who you had a relationship with that you believe would help your life. Why are they no longer in your life? Was the ending of the relationship your fault of was it theirs? Contemplate how your life would have been lived differently if you were still in contact with that person. How would your life be better? What things would you have done? Could you have possibly achieved more of your dreams if you had remained close to them? Or, is the opposite true?

Now, think about how you have behaved in regard to other people. How many people have you reached out to and truly tried to help? Help, with no desired reward? How did those people react to you? Did they appreciate what you attempted to do for them? Or, did they simply take the gesture with no appreciation for what it may have cost your life?

The people we associate with define our lives. Ask yourself, who do you associate with and why? Who did you associate with and why? Where is your life today because of whom you associated with? Where will your life be tomorrow based upon whom you are currently associating with?

Take the time and sincerely isolate the people at the various periods in your life and truly analyze the relationships that you have encountered. Do this because it will provide you with a very important microscope into your life. It will teach you what you have gained from others, what you have given to others, what you have taken from others, how you behave towards others, and how your life has been shaped by the people you have associated with.

Process Verses Evolution
05/May/2020 09:42 AM

There are two very distinct patterns that people follow as they pass through their life. One is pattern. Meaning, they do the things the way they do the things they do and they do them the same way throughout their life. The second is evolution. Meaning, they do what they do but they are constantly attempting to expand on the way they do what they do.

Before we go any father, take a look at your life and while being very honest with yourself, which one of these two categories do you fall into? There is no right or wrong answer; there is simply the way in which you have decided to encounter your life. Do you follow established patterns or do you embrace evolution?

Certainly, doing things the same way is the safest and the easiest, for what is known is known—it is tried and tested. Evolving is harder as it not only takes the mental willingness to expand your level of understanding but it takes your willingness to change.

We can look to many illusions in life to view the process of the choices one makes in how they will encounter life. Perhaps one of the most evident is the way people who embrace the arts encounter their reality. For example, look at the life of a well-known musician. In some cases, you will see (for example) a guitar player who is considered a master of their craft playing the same way in the same style throughout their career. Illustrating that they mastered their craft early in their life and because what they did was appreciated they never took the time to step beyond what they initially accomplished. On the other hand, there are those guitar players who continue to evolve within their chosen vocation and have continued to change, alter, progress, and develop their style of playing as they passed through their life. Again, that does not make one better than the other but it makes one willing to continue their mental and artistic expansion as they pass though their life.

In the martial arts you will see this as well. Particularly in the traditional martial arts you will see an instructor training his (or her) students in a very established manner, most commonly in the same manner as their art was taught to them. There are specific warm-ups, punches, kicks, and katas, all performed in a specific manner that one must do to pass through the various levels of the art. As one progresses they are taught what to do and how to do it in a traditional manner and that is what they teach others once they reach the level of an instructor. This is how the various systems of the traditional martial arts maintain a consistency throughout time. This is not right or wrong; this is just the way it is.

Within this traditional manner of training, however, occasionally a practitioner will decide that they, and what they believe, is a new and better method of doing things. From this comes the birth of a new system of martial arts embracing new techniques that have evolved from what that practitioner has learned. Whereas in the arts, such as painting and music, new innovations are often celebrated. In traditionally based systems such as the martial arts, however, new innovations are often criticized as the traditionalists do not like to witness evolution taking place within their system. This goes forward onto life and is the reason many people stay the same and do not evolve. Evolution is often a revolution. And, a revolution causes a war. Whether that war is on the personal level say between parents and children or friends onto schooling or work environments onto the large social structure on the whole, war equals combat, it also requires a person who is wiling to fight that war and possibly get hurt or lose the battle. Thus, evolution is not easy.

For some, they prefer a life lived in a state of ease, contentment, and no conflict. This is the pathway that most eastern religions embrace. Particularly in modern western culture, however, evolution and revolution has become praised but one must understand there is always a cost.

Some people base their evolution upon overpowering others and defeating the established methods of encountering life. But, is that evolution or is that ego? All the people that want to evolve while stepping over and hurting others do is to create a conflict based upon a self-decided standard that they believe is better. But, a power struggle only leads to conflict and conflict can rarely be seen as something that is good for the all because those who do not wish to be drawn into the conflict must choose a side. Thus, this process is not evolution; it is simply one person deciding that what they think is better than what someone else thinks.

True personal evolution must take place in the person. In must evolve in the person. It must become the person's life signature. Then, if others find it appealing they will choose to make an allegiance with that person. But, even if they do, that does not mean that they are evolving, that simply means that they have chosen a side and a person to follow.

Ultimately, all personal evolution must be made on the personal level. Evolution is not about the greater whole changing, it is about one person changing: becoming better and becoming more.

It is easy to make yourself a follower, because then all of the decisions are made for you. But, any personal evolution must take place within you. It must be you expanding your understanding, your knowledge, and your consciousness.

So, who are you? What life path do you follow? There is no right or wrong answer? Do you follow a process? Or, do you evolve?

*   *   *

05/May/2020 07:14 AM

Does knowing your temperature change the fact that you have a fever?

* * *

04/May/2020 09:25 AM

What are you going to be thinking about when you die?

How Do You Care About Someone You Care About But Someone You Don't Really Know?
01/May/2020 10:09 AM

I was sitting around, taking a moment last evening. I flipped onto one of those channels that offers vintage TV shows. The very first episode of the TV series Adam-12 was just beginning. In the info it showed that the show premiered on September 20, 1968. That was three days before my tenth birthday. I thought back and I was living in Inglewood, California then. My father, who would die exactly three months later, was the Manager of the Los Angeles Forum. I am certain I watched that premiere episode back then, because that's what kids do, watch the new TV shows. But, though I have periodically watched the reruns of the show over the years, I don't believe that I have seen that first episode since then. Interesting, I thought, how the world has changed in many ways but in others, all things are very much the same: people's emotions, their feeling, their hopes, their desires, and their actions and reactions have not changed much at all. That's why I love vintage TV and movies, as they really illustrate a depiction of history.

Anyway... Watching it got me to begin to scan my memory tapes about the evolution of life and how people come and go. Most of the cast members of that show are now gone, as is my family, and many of the people I knew from that era.

The thing about life is that there are those people we know. They are either family members or they are people that we meet, we associate with, and because we like them or grow to care about them we keep them in our lives. This may be for a short amount of time or it may be for years-upon-years. Those people, we know how to react to. They become our family or our friends and through trial and error we can make them know that we care about them—we can let them know that we care about them. But, then there is the entirely different level of being, someone we care about but we are not close to them, we never became family or friends with them but because they have played a part in our life, we want to do something to illustrated that we do care. But, what can we do?

You know, this is a complicated question. For example, iconic religious figures like Jesus or Buddha, there are symbols that we can wear around our neck to illustrate our emotions towards that being. But, what about the everyone else? What about those people that you have appreciated; what they do or what they have said, how do you express to them that you care?

For each of us, there are people that have been a help or an influence to our life. Maybe we listened to their lectures, maybe we read their books, maybe we liked their art, whatever… It really could be anything. But, they helped us. Because we care about the fact that they have helped us, because we consciously acknowledge that they helped us, we want to do something but what can we do?

For me, there were people like Ram Dass as I was growing up who helped me become who I was to become. Though I only met him once or twice, he was a guiding influence in my life in my early years. But, there was really no method to let him know. Of course, there have been others, as well, but for me he is an ideal example.

I believe this is the case for all of us. We can look to a person, a person that we do not know, and we can consciously acknowledge that they helped us on our pathway through life. But, what can we do to do something for them when we do not personally know them? …Because don't you think we should all express our appreciation for someone we like, for someone who has helped us even if we do not personally know them? Isn't that the right thing to do?

Sure, there are the Stalkers out there: physical, internet, or otherwise. I've had a few of those in my days. But, that's just weird. And yes, in this age of technology it is perhaps much easier to communicate with a person off there in the distance than it was in times gone past. But, what can you do to actually do something for a person you care about that you do not really know? I think that's the big question because most people don't do anything. They just sit back in the cut and maybe they appreciate a person in their mind, maybe they like what they say or do, but that's it; all that they feel is locked in their brain.

Think about it. Think about a person who has helped you. What can you do to express your appreciation for their words, their creations, or the what they have done?

Let that be your exercise for today. What can you do to show that you appreciate, that you care about the person who you do not personally know that has helped you or your life in some manner?

Now, I have my ideas… I know some of the things I have done. But, that's me, that's not you. Personally, I think it begin in positivity. Expressing positivity in their direction. Expressing it even if they may never know that you did. But, if you don't do something, then nothing is ever done. If you don't care enough to do anything doesn't that diminish the fact that you actually appreciate that something that someone has given to you?

So, take a few minutes, think it out. Get out there and do something good, something positive for that person who has guided you and/or somehow helped your life; that person that you may not ever personally know. From this, like all things that are based in positivity, all life becomes just a little bit better.

Focusing On Who You Are
30/Apr/2020 09:49 AM

There was a common phrase in use during the counterculture movement of the 1960s into the 1970s, *"I've got to go and find myself."* It was a time when people were trying to become the best version of themselves that they could be. Then came the 1980s and the, *"Me movement,"* where everyone went into debt trying to outdo one another. Different eras, different outcomes, but the conclusion that can be drawn from this is that people are guided by their surrounding influences. If those influences are of a positive, inquisitive nature then the individual and maybe even society on the whole can become better. If, on the other hand, people are only focused on the external nature of life: getting more, being more, and having more, then everything in a person's life and in society as a whole has a tendency to disintegrate.

If we look around us today, we see we are surround by a world of self-promotion. With the dawning of the internet people found a way to make themselves stars. Though there is certainly nothing wrong with this, and it is simply a depiction of our time in history, but what has come out of this is a focus on the self; i.e. the lower self, but not the higher self.

People want to become. People want to be that, *"Something."* For the people who don't see themselves as good enough to become, *"Something,"* they then fall into the pattern of worshiping those people who do.

Think about modern society in today's world. Think about how many people place themselves in front of a camera and broadcast on YouTube or other sites doing nothing, saying nothing, and achieving nothing of real importance. Fly on an airplane and you can witness the young woman watching how-to make-up presentations. Talk to people, ask them what they do, and many will speak about the personalities they watch online.

But, how does learning how to do your make-up lead to a better life? How does it lead to a better world? How does watching a person talk about playing video games or discussing the creations of others make their life or the life of anyone else any more?

Throughout history there have always been the leaders and there have been the followers. There has also always been the people who hate the leaders and hate the followers. But, whatever the feeling, what does any of this hold for the growth of the individual? How does it make them a better, more complete, more whole, more conscious, more caring individual? How does it make them a better person? Are they trying to find themselves or are they simply taking the drug of oblivion—the elixir of thinking about nothing and/or allowing their emotions to control their every thought.

There are the people that do. There have always been the people that do. They create. Whether that creation is achieved through science, biology, physics, art, or spirituality, they are creating a new something or at least a new interpretation of that something. Then there is the everybody else.

The fact of life is, not everyone is a doer; not everyone is a creator. And, that's fine. That's life. But, if a person does not care enough to actually take the time to try to make themselves the best that they can be then their life eventually comes to equal nothing. They are simply being guided by the winds of time and the minds of those people who understand that they can control the minds of other if they place themselves upon center stage.

So, who are you? Do you know the answer to that question? Do you ever actually consciously ponder that question? Are you a creator or are you a follower? Are you a teacher or are you a student? But, more importantly, why are you what you are? Why are you doing what you do?

Each day, you need to ask yourself, what are you doing today to make yourself a more whole, understanding, conscious, caring, giving, and complete individual? What are you doing to make you the person who helps other people? You also need to ask yourself is what you are doing simply designed to waste your time? Ask yourself, who are you looking to and who are you listening to. Is what they are saying making your reality and the reality of anyone else any better? Or, are they only doing what they do to make themselves feel better about their life as they create a flock of followers?

We all need distractions. We all need hobbies. We all need to make a living. But, if we do not take the time to find our true placement in our reality, if we don't take the time to, "Find ourselves," and understand where we belong and what we should truly be doing in life, then all the doing of nothing will only come to a life defined by doing nothing.

Take the time to learn who you truly are. Avoid wasting your life. Avoid listening to people who waste your life and guide you down the road of distraction and/or negativity. Become the best you that you can become. ...It takes work. ...It takes conscious focus. But, if you do not try, all you will become is the shadow of what you should have been.

Your life is defined, created, and lived by you. Your life has the potential to influence everyone else on this planet. What are you going to do with it?

Telling the Truth
29/Apr/2020 04:08 PM

Let's fact facts, a lot of people lie. A lot of people disguise the truth. A lot of people hide the truth. A lot of people stretch the truth. A lot of people make up a lot of things.

There is really no reason to go into why people lie because each person who lies has their own reason for doing so. Whether that reason is also a lie is a whole other issue but I think we can leave it to say, a lot of people lie about a whole lot of things. Some even fight to get their lies to be believed.

The problem with people lying is, because they are a liar, most of those liars think everyone else is lying as well. They know they don't tell the truth, so they assume and accuse other people of lying just as they do. Some even accuse other people of lying to cover up the lies that they have told.

Have you ever lied? Why did you lie? How did that lie come to define and affect your life?

How do you feel about the lies that you've told? Do those lies bother you? Do you ever think or care about how those lies have affected the lives of other people? If you don't, what does that say about you as a human being?

Once you lied were you afraid of getting caught in your lie? Did you get caught in your lie? If you did, how did that affect your life?

Some people never get caught in the lies they have told. They live their entire existence based upon a lie they told years and years ago. They get away with it. But, simply because a person gets away with telling a lie—and even if that lie comes to be believed, does that change the fact that it was not the truth? And, if a person basis their life upon a lie—if they succeed because of a lie, what does that say about the foundation of their life and any success they may have achieved? Moreover, what does that say about all of the people who came to believe their lie?

Most people want to believe what another person is saying. This is why some people are allowed to define their entire life based upon a lie.

Some people believe the lies that they tell other people. But, simply because someone has come to believe the lie they originated does it ever become the truth?

The truth is easy. It may not be pretty, it may not be eloquent, but it is the truth.

A lie is messy. A lie is forever a problem because a lie is never the truth and there is always the possibility that the truth will be revealed.

We can all understand that all people should only speak the truth but that will probably never happen as people want to be seen as more, people want to have achieved more, and people want what they want and they are willing to lie to get what they want.

What does this tell us about life? It tells us that as long as we base our life upon the truth, as long as we always speak the truth, at least our part of life will remain honest.

It's important to note that telling the truth is not you telling someone what you think about them for all that kind of mind stuff is simply based in judgment, emotions, and ego. The truth of the truth goes much deeper than all of that, "What you think and feel," kind of stuff. The truth is what you have actually done, what you have actually lived, what you truly are and who you truly are. The truth is you being true about yourself and to yourself.

A person can lie about who they are all they want. They can lie about what they truly do and what they have truly done. A person can live their entire life based upon the falsehoods of self-imagination, self-projection, and self-proclamation but if they do that, at the end of their days, they will never know the truth as their life has been an expression of a lie.

So, next time you think about lying, catch yourself, and don't do it. For there is nothing that you will truly gain by lying. The next time someone lies to you, smile, know that what they are saying is emanation from a lower level being who is lost in their own self-projection of a false reality and walk away. You don't have to call them a liar; you just do not have to believe them.

If you live the truth, then you are the truth, as plain, as simply, and as boring as that truth may be. If you live the truth, though you may never be seen as some great, grand, representation of someone who lives at the pinnacle of all that is desired but, at least, you will never be known as a liar.

Artificial Intelligence
27/Apr/2020 09:47 AM

In a world where everyone spouts off their mouth about what they think is right, who they think is wrong, and what they think about the whatever they think about, there is so much personalized bullshit being spouted and presented as actually knowledge, why should you listen to anyone?

Fact Check:

Is what someone is saying based upon factual knowledge or is it their onion about what someone else did, said, or created? If what someone is talking about is based upon what someone else did, said, or created all that person is doing is voicing their opinion. Is an opinion fact? No. It is just what someone thinks about what someone else did. If opinion is not fact, why you should listen to what they have to say? Because opinions vary. You have yours, I have mine, and other people have theirs. But, an opinion is never a fact.

Do you ever consciously define where a person's opinion is rising from when you listen to them speak? Most people do not. This is why so many outspoken people are allowed to build a flock of followers that, in many cases, is the source of their livelihood. Most people do not have the ability to think for themselves and because of this fact, they believe whomever is saying whatever it is they are saying, simply because they are saying it.

There are some people who truly hold the credentials for what they teach. They have gone to school, they have earned the degrees, they have worked in their field, and they have gained the respect of those people who formalize the curriculum in that field. Those people at least can speak from a position of authority in that they aspired, they studied, they earned the degree, and then they were provided with the credentials to teach. Most of the people who speak, especially those who wish to loudly voice their opinion, are not like this, however. They have just develop the ability to speak and unleash their opinions based upon a mindset of all-knowing ego and from this they then place themselves on the pulpit with no credentials to back up what they are saying. In many ways, these people do the most damage to this life space and to anyone who will listen to them because all they have done is to develop a pool of blind followers who do not possess the ability to cut through the opinion-based factual inaccuracies and think for themselves.

So, what does this tell us about life? What it tells us is that if we listen to people simply because we like what they have to say or the way they say it—if we listen to people who do nothing more than base what they say upon opinion, then we are removing the truth from our life. If we do this, we are allowing ourselves to have our emotions and our actions guided by those who do not deserve to possess that ability of control.

If you're going to listen to someone, if you are going to believe what they say without first researching the basis of their facts, know that you have given the true essence of your being away—you have handed it over to someone who does nothing more then tell the world what they think about someone or something else.

Does what you think about someone else or what that someone else has done really matter? Does what you think about that someone or that something else actually change reality on any level? A true life is based upon a true perspective. A true perspective can only be had by internal self-realization. The only way to achieve that is to remove all of the false influences from your mind, hone your own factual understating about reality, and move forward through your life based upon an understand of fact but never opinion.

Getting an Actor to Act the Way You Want Them to Act
26/Apr/2020 09:33 AM

For each of us, I am sure that we have been watching a movie or a TV show and we notice that an actor is not really hitting their mark in terms of their performance. They are there, spitting out the lines, but they are doing so in a manner that we feel is incorrect.

It is the supposed job of Director's, on the set of a film, to guide the actors in providing the performance that they want. So, when an actor is not hitting his or her mark, whose fault is it: the actor or the director?

There are some people who believe they possess the ability to judge the performances of actors. Some of these people are professional reviewers while others are simply armchair quarterbacks. Whatever the case, everyone interprets what they see on the screen based upon their own unique set of desires and standards.

As a director, myself, I know what it is actually like on a set. This is something that many of the people who unleash criticism do not truly understand. For me, as a director, I try to work with people who I understand their abilities and their limitations. From this, I can anticipate what style of performance I will get out of them. Thus, if it is ever necessary, I can simply give them a minimal amount of guidance and they will give their best performance; at least in terms of my vision for their character.

But, this is not always possible. Sometimes a director is blindsided by an actor's ego, distain, negative attitude, or inability to provide the expected performance due to some other reason. I think back to a very funny event that took place when we were filming the Zen Film, *Shotgun Blvd.,* which later evolved into, *Armageddon Blvd.* The great old-school actor Conrad Brooks was part of the cast. There was a bit of time that we did not need him on the set which was on our stages in the historic Broadway Building on Hollywood and Vine., so he and his protégé walked over to a nearby bar, *The Frolic Room,* where they a few drinks. When he came back, we were ready to shoot his character's scenes. The thing was, due to the fact that he had his buzz on, he could not remember any of the lines we feed him. Literally, he could not remember more than a few words at a time.

The problem was, my character was to act with him, as were a couple of other people. Conrad, who was a GREAT guy, had totally checked out. But, we needed to get the scenes shot. Plus, he wanted to do his stuff, but he could not.

We were befuddled for a bit but then we finally had an idea, we had one of our actors, Roger Ellis, (who appeared in several of my films), tell him his lines one sentence at a time. Roger would say the line, Conrad would repeat it with a few different inflections, and we got the scenes shot. Editing that stuff was a pain in the ass but Conrad's scenes got put on film. His performance was etched in that great old-style of acting that he embraced, based in cinema of times gone past.

Does anyone who sees the film understand the process that it took to create that film? No. At least, not if they weren't there. Does any critic know the subtle unspoken reality of any actor's performance they analyze or the reality of what it took to create any film they criticize? Nope. They just see what they see, judge it as they will, but never understand the underlying reality of its process of creation. And, that is sad. It fact it is just wrong.

So, what does this tell us about life? It tells us that there are the subtle elements that take place in the creation and the living of each of our lives. There are the things that we must do to make our life happen. There are things that we must work out— actions that we much figure out to make the scenes of our life take place. And, no one but us knows these things. So, whenever you think you know something about someone, whenever you judge someone, whenever you think that someone is doing something wrong and they should be doing it a different way, rethink that thought and realize you do not truly know anything about that person's reality and/or what they had to do to do whatever it is they did.

* * *
26/Apr/2020 08:27 AM

If you won't apologize to the people that you've hurt what does that say about you as a human being?

* * *

24/Apr/2020 03:49 PM

Just because someone is willing to give doesn't mean that you should do the taking.

Pictures of the Past
24/Apr/2020 03:23 PM

In life, we all get older. That is just the name of the name. …We get older until we die.

In life, we all interact with people. We know them. We know what they look like. We know them until we do not know them anymore.

In life, people move on. You see a person—you associate with a person, you do that until you don't do that anymore. Again, that is just the name of the game.

In life—in our life, we know what a person looked like when we knew them. This is the image that we keep in our mind. Though we may have known them one year, ten years, twenty years, fifty years ago, we remember them as we knew them. We remember them as they were.

In life, every now and then, we see one of those people that we knew, way back in the way back when. Maybe it is via a photograph or maybe we bump into them. But, who they are now is not who they were then. With age, the beauty of youth fades. … Just the name of the game.

In life, some how this is all really sad when we re-meet that person. Sure, we too have grown older. But, we know that. We look in the mirror every day. We know what we look like. We know what they people we see everyday look like. But, don't see someone over a long person of time and then see them; BAM, reality strikes. What they are is not what they were. They have gotten old.

In life, a lot of people fight the aging process. For some it works. For others it just makes them look worse. But, the reality of the reality is, there is no fighting the curse of time. We are not what we were yesterday.

In life, all we can really do is prepare ourselves. Prepare

ourselves for what we are to become and prepare ourselves for the fact of what others have become. When you see them, try not to be too shocked.

Tick tock, you're getting old.

*   *   *

23/Apr/2020 04:47 PM

People are always excited when they get away with doing something illegal but they want the villain to pay the maximum penalty when someone does something illegal to them.

Literary Fragments
23/Apr/2020 10:04 AM

For anyone who has ever written literature or other stuff, you understand that though you may start many stories, you do not finish all of them. There's probably a million reasons for this but whatever that reason is, not all starts find a finish.

Back in the 80s, with the dawning of the first generation of home computers, I was writing a lot of poetry, short stories, and novels. Many of them found a publisher. Though a lot of the novels and stories were completed, there were a few that just stopped. For whatever reasoning and/or logic I had at the time, I never finished them.

As the age of the old DOS and other early language computers faded away, luckily I printed out all of those stories that were in various forms of completion on one of those loud typewriter style printers. Maybe twenty years ago I had the idea that I should publish all of those partially finished tales just as they stood. Yes, I could probably go back into them and finish them if I wanted to, but then was then and it seemed better that I did not go back into them as so much time had passed and so much in my life had changed. Up until this point in time I never got around to that task, however. I've been busy! And, maybe I still will not. But recently, I pull out the folder that held those unfinished novels. I did an OCR scan of the first one I pulled out, Surgery of the Soul. So, for the whatever it's worth, here it is, the foundations of a Scott Shaw novel that was never competed.

Surgery of the Soul

By Scott Shaw, Ph.D.

To:
Denise and Judy

for all of the right reasons

To:
Xiao Ling, Li Fu, and Tiffany
for all of the wrong ones

Chapter Uno

I ride through the rolling lush green hills of Southern China like a king in heat. I sit in the rear of a four-door sedan, dark blue in color, tinted windows in the back. I am accompanied by my bodyguard. In the front rides my driver, solo.

No, his name is not Solo; not like Napoleon Solo, like, you know, from the 60's T.V. series, The Man From Uncle. He just rides up front, solo. Name, well awh… Damn, that doesn't really mean that much now does it? He doesn't really play that much of an important roll in the tale I am about to spin anyway.

But, it was all like a dream; a fucking dream if you don't mind my using my native L.A. slang. Sooner or later slang always seems to become the norm, anyway.

The road passed in front of us. In front, soon to be in our rear, as the pagan green hills, covered with blooming life existed, dominating my field of vision, I was swept to dreams of the love that must be waiting for me here; lost into the dreams of all that this place holds for me, this Southern place/space.

China… Of ALL that it owed me, having been tossed out on my ear, psychologically and heart broken. What was it now, four years ago? But that was another tale, told in another book. And, the past, never repeats itself. Or does it?

I looked out across the green horizon; passing the so-called peasants working the fields; wearing large round, pointed topped hats, just like in the movies; realizing that it would have been a far better thing for China never to have opened the bamboo curtain at all, never to have tried to keep up with the modern western world; far better to have been alone, isolated, where the people would never have known the difference; lost to another glance in another chance.

As the castles of the former War Lords stood out and stared above the walls of civilization, in all of their ambivalent grayness; reminiscent of a different, a darker time, lost to its own suchness of nothingness. I was living a dream; and this dream that had to happen. I would not allow it to be any other way.

The passion stocked me. It forced its embrace upon me. Like the lips that had found mine, the day I left L.A. For out here on the outskirts, a million miles into the land of never-never, that too meant nothing. This is the place that held it all.

Green, the most mystical of colors, pounded my vision. The rice fields, where the people walked, planting their substance, the gray profoundness of the castles of power.

This was the land where Lao Tsu had walked. And now, it was mine; my playground.

As the warm Spring heat pounded onto the countryside surrounding me, engulfing me, even in some ways controlling me, I was lost to its omnipresence. I was contained, self-contained inside the dark blue auto in which I rode. I had a driver, a bodyguard, air conditioning, money in my pocket, a desire in my heart, and the green passive purity of passing pagan China, complete with its peasants outside of me, stroking my field of vision.

A car, a driver, a desire; her name Li Fu; Chinese, golden Southern China skin: a green card in one eye, a dollar sign in the other, but I did not care. I had seen those eyes before, felt this desire one too many times to really care. I stared deep into myself, looking for a feeling, realizing that there should be one when there was not. I mean like, here I was on the other side of the world, other side of the world from where I was the week previous. I look, I studied, as the scenery passed, as the desires passed, as I wondered, knowing I should be feeling something,

something more, something different, something about the here and the now; in a life that passes all too briefly. In studying, in looking, in the trying to care, I realized that there was nothing, that I felt nothing different, that I was nothing different. Nothing more than I was a week ago bound in L.A. Nothing more than I was years ago, when my feet were first placed upon this soil. God damn, like there must be something, but there was not. Just the passing green, a driver who didn't care; no not really, a body guard, only in it for the pay, for the prestige, a babe waiting hotel side, desirous of any *"gui-lo,"* (white boy) that may come along and show an interest. Who was the fool?

So, I guess I did it, gave you all of the specific in the first chapter, all of the games that would be played, all of the feelings that may be held, all of the nothing about to unfold. But, the games and the dance go on and on, and hey, like, all of this dancing does make a story. A story from HELL perhaps? A lot of times, life; it does look better, feel better, on the words upon a page, on the pictures upon a screen.

Read on...

Where Do Your Thoughts Come From?
22/Apr/2020 07:43 AM

Each person thinks pretty much all of the time that they are awake. The mind is constantly thinking. From one thought onto the next, the mind is rarely silent. But, where do thoughts come from? Where do your thoughts come from? Do you ever take the time to follow your thoughts to their sourcepoint?

Most people simply think. Though each person thinks differently, there is a certain common pattern of thought defined by where a person was born, indoctrinated, educated, lived, and their time and placement in history. Beyond that, each person creates a pattern of thought that they actualize throughout their life.

Ponder this… Are your thoughts—is your pattern of thinking any different from it was five years ago, ten years ago, twenty years ago? Certainly, what you focus your thoughts upon may have changed but has how you think changed? The answer to this question is, probably not as people establish a pattern of thinking and then they occupy that pattern of thinking throughout their life.

But, more to the point, ask yourself, "where do your thoughts come from?" Do you ever take the time to isolate a thought that you are having and follow it to its source? Do you ever analyze that thought and find out where it came from and why you are thinking it? If you don't, then you really don't know yourself. You are simply being guided by what you think. But, if you don't know what you are thinking, or why you are thinking it, then you can never possess any true sense of self-awareness.

Focusing on and analyzing a specific thought is most easily done when your mind is in a state of rest. This can be accomplished during meditation. It can also happen in a more natural state like when you are just waking up in the morning or are going to bed a night.

The process of tracing a thought to its source is quite easy. You simply have to first isolate a thought and then follow that thought back to its origin. Question, why are you thinking that thought, what was the first time you thought that thought, what is the impetus of that thought, is it based on something you heard, something you felt, something someone told you, or is it based upon something you previously thought?

For each person they can develop their own process of analysis and develop the ability to understand the sourcepoint of their thoughts. Follow a thought to its source and then you can understand the origin of that thought. From there, you can come to a clearer understand of not only why you are thinking what you are thinking but a clearer understanding of how your thoughts have caused you to act and react throughout your life.

Know the source of your thoughts. Understand why you are thinking what you are thinking. Do this, and you can come to truly understanding the essence of your being.

* * *

22/Apr/2020 07:41 AM

How much suffering have you alleviated?

Pandemic Protests and What Does a Gun Have to Do with the Coronavirus?
21/Apr/2020 03:18 PM

If you've been watching the news recently, during this time of COVID-19 Coronavirus, you will certainly have seen how some people have been getting antsy about being forced to stay at home. Most people understand that this is for the betterment of the greater whole—to keep people from getting sick and dying. Others, however, don't care. They want to go back out in the out and about, do their jobs, have their haircuts and their nails done, go shopping, go to the gym, so on and so forth...

Over the past several days there have actually been protests erupting in cities across the country. In these protests, many of the participants were not doing the suggested social distancing, wearing protective masks, or anything like that. Okay... Not smart or safe but this is the United States and you can legally protest if you don't like something even if the thing you are protesting against is designed to make the all and the everyone more safe.

In some of the protests, in some of the states where the gun carry laws are more relaxed, you see these guys walking around with their AKs across their chest, their shotguns in their hands, and their side arms in full view. Again, okay... If it's legal, it's legal. My question is, however, what does carrying a gun have to do with a pandemic protest? What is the purpose? What is the need to carry a gun to a protest rally simply because you don't like the stay at home suggestion?

For the record, I am a gun owner and a supporter of the 2nd Amendment. As an actor, I've used guns as props in some of the films I've acted in. But, that's all pretend. That's not real life. But, what these people are doing is taking place in real life. Again, what is the purpose? What is the need to carry a gun to a protest rally simply because you don't like the stay at home suggestion?

I think there are a lot of people out there who do not possess a clear sense of Self. A lot of people want to come off like the actors in the big action films who save the day by blowing people away. But, that's pretend. That's not real life. If you want to carry a gun and you want to be a true hero, why don't you go join the military? You don't need to show off the guns you own at a political protest just to make yourself believe that you look cool and you are somehow all-powerful. That's just childish.

No matter what leader or which political party is in power, there is always going to be those people who agree with the powers that be and their policies and there will be those who don't. All good... That's life. There are going to be national and local declaration made that some people will agree with and others will not. That's fine. That's life. But, though many would say that a protest is nothing more than a staged presentation, political theater, that does not mean that people need to bring their weapons to the rally because a protest will not (or at least should not) end up being a shoot out.

A man doesn't need a gun to be a man. A woman doesn't need a gun to be a woman. If you disagree with something, protest. In the United States, that's your right. But, just like the guy who drives a flashy car to try to make himself look cool or important, someone who carries a gun, and doesn't do it for immediate self-protection, just makes himself or herself look bad.

You don't need a gun to be perceived as a strong individual.

Relationship Tells
21/Apr/2020 07:42 AM

Each of our lives is based upon the relationships that we have. Many of our life-actions are enacted due to the people we are associating with. Relationship are one of the most defining and essential factors in our lives, yet how much time do you spend actually analyzing the people you are in relationships with?

There is a saying in gambling. It is particularly used in association with poker. It is called a, *"Tell." "A Tell,"* is the way a person commonly behaves when they have a specific hand. It is a subtle face movement or physically gesture that they do when they believe they have a winning hand or perhaps a losing hand. In life, people have, *"Tells,"* as well. Each person has a pattern of behavior and very few people ever change the way they behave or alter the way in which they react throughout their life.

Think about a time when you met a person. Maybe you liked them, you were attracted to them, you thought they were an interesting person, maybe you even wanted to gain something from being in a relationship with them. But, as you got to know them you begin to notice a trait in their character or behavior that you did not really like. Perhaps you made excuses for that trait that they possessed and you remained in association with them. As you went through your time together did that trait ever go away? Probably not. If it was a good trait, all was fine. But, if it was a bad trait it probably came to not only negatively affect your relationship with the person but it may have actually damaged your life.

So, if you saw that trait, if you identified that trait, if you knew they had it, if you did not like it, why did you hang out with them in the first place?

Relationships fall apart all the time. They disintegrate for many reasons. Mostly, they collapse because one person doesn't like what the other person is doing or has done. But, think about it, think about your life, think about the relationships that you have had that you have left; couldn't you just have saved everyone a lot of time and trouble if you didn't get into them in the first place?

Some relationships, like family, we are forced into. Some relationships, like the ones we have at work, we must tolerate. But, all the other relationships are a choice. And, if you do not study who you are in association with or if you study them, know their flaws, and hang out with them anyway, who's fault is it when everything goes awry?

* * *

21/Apr/2020 07:42 AM

How much of what you are thinking is actually important compared to how much of what you are thinking is simply rambling thoughts based upon the fact that you do not have anything more important to focus upon?

What Do You Want for Christmas?
19/Apr/2020 08:55 AM

As we pass through this period of pandemic, many of us have been locked inside our homes much more than is normal. In states like California, we have the, *"Safer at home,"* order in place. And, it's true. It's scary outside. You go out there and you could catch this coronavirus, get sick and die. Nobody wants that. When I go to the supermarket everyone is masked up, some people are also wearing gloves. That's when it really took hold for me. From one day to the next, it was like walking into one those futuristic movies where everyone is controlled by this dark sinister force.

People are at home. Some are very concerned about their finances, as they are not getting paid. How about you? Others are concerned that they will not have enough food to feed their family because they have no money. How about you? Some people are worried about the fact that they could not pay their rent? How about you? With all this, the government, at least here in California (and other places), has put this thing into place where a landlord can't evict tenants, during this pandemic, if they don't pay their rent. There are protests taking place about, *"Free rent."* But, what about the landlords when the tenants don't pay their rent and because of that fact they can't pay their mortgage? The bank is going to take over their property. So, pretty much everybody is screwed one way or the other. If you are finically set, with your rent paid and food on your table, consider yourself very-very lucky. ...But, do you? Do you ever think about how lucky you are?

Scrolling around the social websites, I see a lot of people asking for suggestions about what they should do while they are stuck at home? What series on Netflix is good? What movies to watch? And, stuff like that? On the news stations they are giving people at home workout tips and DIY ideas. This is all fine and good but...

Mostly, what a lot of people are doing, meaning those who are not in crisis and/or are not sick, is either wasting time, finding a way to waste time, or contemplating what they will do when this pandemic is over—if it ever is. What they are doing is thinking about themselves. How about you?

If we look a society; if we study the world and human nature on the whole, this is what most people do most of the time. They think about themselves. If they are not a trained something: like a doctor, a nurse, a paramedic, and the like, they are thinking about themselves. If they are not a professional, where their mind must be focused on their company, they are thinking about themselves. If they are not happy with the actions of the government and are not out there protesting, they are thinking about themselves. How about you? What are you thinking about right now? What did you think about yesterday? What did you think about last night? What did you think about when you woke up this morning? And, how does what you are currently thinking about compare to what you were thinking about six months ago, before this pandemic took hold of the world?

As is understood in the philosophy of Buddhism, Right Thought equals Right Action. So, what are you thinking about? And, how is what you are thinking about causing you to act?

In life, you can spend your time thinking about anything that you want. In life, you can allow what you think to guide your actions. But, what has what you thought caused you do? …What has it caused you to do lately? Are you focusing on figuring out what Netflix series to watch or are you focusing on how you can have better thoughts and thereby become a better person. Are you focusing on what you can do for someone else that will make a positive difference in their life?

Life is all about choice. Your life is all about your choices. What choice are you going to make? Are you going to spend your time in a state of mental angst, floating from one selfish and self-serving time-killing thought to the next or are you going to make a choice, refining your thinking and decide what you can do to help the life of someone else—to give them what they want for Christmas instead of just thinking about what you want?

You Can't Make Someone Become What They Can't Become
18/Apr/2020 03:25 PM

For each of us, we have hopes for other people. Maybe it is a friend, maybe it is a family member, maybe it someone we are attracted to, maybe it is someone we are in a relationship with, maybe it is someone we just met, maybe it is a student, you name it… We know a person and we hope, we believe, that they can become something more than what they already are.

Maybe this something more has to do with physical training. Maybe it has to do with emotional behavior. Maybe it is something that we want them to change that we don't like in them. Maybe we want them to behave in a manner we find more appealing. Whatever it is, it is us who wants them to do or become something other than what they currently are.

In life, some people try to be better. They work very hard at becoming more. Others do not. They are locked into a place: be it physical or mental and they remain trapped there for their rest of their life. Though there are a million reasons why some people do not desire to change, the fact is, no matter how much you or I may want them to become something else, due to their emotional foundations, they cannot change.

Then, there are those who we see, we talk to, we suggest, we teach, and for them they truly try and try to become that something that we hoped they could be. They try, but, no matter how they try, it is all to no avail. They simply do not possess the physical or the psychological make up to become what we believe they can become.

There is one problem in the mindset of hoping someone will change, however. That is the mindset of us projection what we want, expect, or desire onto someone else. This, by its very nature, is hurtful to the something that person already is. It is telling them that they are not enough—that they are not yet good enough. But, who are any of us to judge anyone?

So, the next time you find yourself thinking someone should be something else—should do anything else, remind yourself, you can't make someone become what they can't become.

If you allow a person to be the perfect representation of who they are by their own definition, everyone in the world becomes that much more emancipated.

Gifts That You Don't Want
17/Apr/2020 01:38 PM

I think we are all pretty happy when we receive a gift that we really want. There are also the times when we get an unexpected gift that we really like or we can really use and we are happy that a person cared about us enough to give it to us. But then, there are those other gifts—gifts that you get that you really don't want and you really don't know what to do with. Those are the strange ones. They are strange because the person who gave it to you was nice enough to care about you to the degree that they gave you a gift. But, now you've got it. What do you do with it?

There is this over-the-shoulder leather brief case style bag I bough at a thrift store a couple of years back. I got it to carry papers, a laptop, and stuff like that when I'm riding my motorcycle. I don't use it too much but it is one of those things that I keep around incase it is needed. It hangs on a hook on the back of my bedroom door along with my travel backpack so I see it all the time. It is one of those items that though you know it's there, you don't really pay it too much attention. Passing it to today, however, it somehow touched a place in my memory and made me remember this kind of interesting/strange situation about receiving a gift that I didn't really want.

After my *Zen Filmmaking* brother, Donald G. Jackson passed away, his wife and daughter were hit with the cold hard reality of the fact that their landlord of the house they had rented for over twenty years asked them to move. Don was a massive hoarder, so his wife and daughter had to get rid of all of his enormous amount of stuff in thirty days. I can't even imagine what that must have felt like after just losing your husband/father. I helped his wife as much as I could by coming by a couple of times a week and carting off all kinds of Don's junk to thrift stores and places like that.

...I discuss this a bit in the book I recently put together

about the life and the filmmaking career of Donald G. Jackson, *Soldier of Cinema*...

Anyway... Passing by my over-the-shoulder bag this morning it got me to remembering this one situation that took place between DGJ and myself many years ago. We had a suite at the American Film Market, as we did each year, offering our movies for sale to the national and international market. We had hired a couple of sellers to do the grunt work but the deal was whoever sold a film would get ten percent of the price they negotiated as a commission. One day this buyer from Malaysia came in and he wanted one of our films. None of the sales people were around so I ended up selling him the film for Malaysia distribution. The next day, Don cashed the check the guy had written us.

We were walking around the Santa Monica promenade, which is not far from where AFM is held, and Don saw this bag being sold by one of the sellers from their kiosk. It was this big ugly black leather over-the-shoulder bag that someone had attached a bunch of pieces of car license plates to. Again, really ugly. The kind of stuff Don liked. The price of the bag was close to five hundred dollars. What a waste of money! But, Don bought it. After he did, he realized that the five hundred dollars he had in his pocket was my commission. *"I think I just spent your commission,"* Don said in a smart assed fashion.

I never got paid that five hundred dollars, which really pissed me off, because I'm not a salesman! I didn't want to do the deal. I just did it to keep up our creditability, as none of the salespeople were around when the buyer showed up. But, since I did, I deserved to be paid for it! Time went on and that whole situation faded with time...

Move forward several years and I am helping Don's wife get ready for their move. We were in their garage, digging through stuff, and his wife came upon the bag. Upon finding it, she immediately gave it to me. It was such a strange experience, because here was this bag that I thought was really ugly and Don had purchased with my commission. I never saw it after the day it bought it. He never used. But, here it was being given to me. I didn't want it but I knew Don's wife had to clear out all of his stuff so I took it never telling her the story of how it came into his possession. Her heart was certainly in the right place for giving it to me. And, in some weird way, I guess I finally got paid my commission.

So, here's the question(s), when you are put in one of those situations; what do you do with a gift that you don't want? What is the most conscious thing you can do?

Some people are really unappreciative of getting a gift they don't want. They make the giving-person feel bad for their giving. But, that's just wrong. If nothing else, you should at least relish in the fact that they cared enough about you to give you something in the first place. Thank them. Let them know you appreciate their giving.

But, then comes the question of what do you do with the gift that you don't want? What can you consciously do to appreciate the receiving of the gift? …In terms of the bag, what was I supposed to do with it? As I am one of those people who is constantly cleansing and moving the energy of, "Stuff," along, I didn't want keep it even though it did hold an interesting spot in my memories of DGJ. I asked my lady if she knew anyone she wanted to give it to? No… So me, I donated it to a thrift store. I figured at least that way it will get into the hands of someone who really likes it. It was my way of moving the, "Giving," along, even if I will never know who ultimate received it. …I hope who ever ended up with the bag enjoyed my five hundred dollar commission payment?

*   *   *
16/Apr/2020 05:53 PM

What if every lie were true?

* * *

16/Apr/2020 09:14 AM

Everyone remembers what you owe them.

Everyone forgets what they owe you.

Accusations Are a Dangerous Game
15/Apr/2020 09:36 AM

If you look around the world today, if you listen to the talking heads on the news channels, the voices on talk radio, or the typing hands on the internet, there is a lot of accusations flying around. A lot of people are saying a lot of things about someone else.

Some people are very bold in their statements. They threaten. They exclaim. They promise to tell the world some dark secret about some other person. But, they are not that person. As they are not that person they do not truly know who or what that person is or why they have done what they done. In fact, via limited, biased research (if any at all) they are only presenting dogma from their personal perspective. This is all very dangerous and it can be very damming as many people do not posses the developed ability to seek the truth on their own. They are simply lazy. They wish to believe anything that suits their predetermined interpersonal definitions.

People have opinions. That is human nature. Some people fight to have their opinions believed. Some people decide that they don't like a person, for any number of self-motivated reasons, and they set about on a course to damage the reality of that person by casting accusations. A very low level of human existence, yes, but one that is put into practice all the time.

Take a look at your current reality. Take a look at this current reality. Identify all of the accusations that you are currently hearing or reading. Do you ever question the source of the information a person who is unleashing the accusations is referencing? Do you ever question the personal bias of the person who is unleashing the accusations? Do you ever question why they are doing it in the first place and how what they are doing will be a benefit to them? If you don't, you are as much a part of the problem as is the individual who is throwing the accusations.

How much of an accusation is fact and how much of an accusation is based upon the interpretation(s) of the person who is casting the accusation?

Why do you choose to believe what you believe? Why do you believe what other people say? Why do you choose to define your thoughts, your emotions, and your life reactions based upon the accusations of any individual, no matter how true they claim their accusations to be?

It is easy for a person to throw out accusations. People can say anything that they want, be it truth or a lie. People can claim sourcing for their accusations. But, what is the ultimate truth of anything? Does that not only exist in the reality of the individual person?

People can easily throw out accusations. The people who do this are commonly attempting to keep any focus or scrutiny off of themselves. By throwing out accusations, they keep the focus on someone else.

Do you ever take the time to think about the lies and/or dark deeds the person who is casting accusations may have committed? Do you ever wonder why they are taking the time to create the accusations in the first place?

Sure, they may be able to give you a hundred reasons why they are saying what they are saying about whomever they are saying it about. But, who are they? What is their hidden truth? What is their agenda? What are they hiding? Why are they focusing on anyone else but making themselves a better person? And, why are they taking the time to say what they are saying in the first place? Ask yourself these questions before you ever believe what anyone is saying.

To quote a well-known biblical passage, John 8:7 *"And as they continued to ask him, he stood up and said to them, 'Let he who is without sin among you be the first to throw a stone at her.'"*

Out of Respect
14/Apr/2020 01:52 PM

In the martial arts, the practitioners are always taught to respect one another. You treat your teacher with respect, you treat your fellow students with respect, and you also treat other practitioners with respect. Respect is at the heart of the teachings of the true martial arts.

Most people never go through formal martial art training, however. Thus, most people are never taught the formalized level of integrity that is required to truly embrace a life defined by honor, reverence, and respect. Most people simply exist in a realm of disrespect, believing that they can say or do anything that they want and behave any way they wish with little or no consequences. This has especially become the case since the dawning of the internet age, where most everyone is nothing more than a faceless screen name.

Currently, in these days of coronavirus COVID-19, people are being asked to take other people into consideration. ...To respect them. For example, in the city of Los Angeles, and many other cities in California and around the country and the world, people are now required to wear face masks. Though the wearing of face masks does not actually provide one with absolute projection from acquiring the disease, they are designed so that people do not spread the disease as readily.

Southern California, and particularly the greater Los Angeles area, is broken up into numerous small cities that form the larger whole. Each of the cities has their own laws and regulation, and in some cases, their own police force. In the city where I live, the requirement to wear a face mask is not mandatory, though most people, out of respect for others, do wear them. As do I when I am in a public place.

I was in the supermarket this morning and virtually everyone was wearing a face mask. But, there were a few people who were arrogantly strutting down the isles open faced.

In life, it is not unusual to interact with people who only think about themselves. But, there is something really wrong with this style of behavior. It doesn't matter who you are, how much money you do or do not have, or how you compare yourself to other people. What matters is how you treat other people for that is the ultimate definition of a life. What matters is the level of respect you show other people.

Not everyone is trained in a discipline such as the martial arts where respect is expected. And, that is sad, because when you are trained in the study of respect, you truly come to understand that other people matter. Other people are important. Other people deserve respect.

So, for all you martial artists (or non-martial artists) out there, let me suggest that you practice respect. Give other people the respect that they deserve. I am sure you wish to be treated in a respectful matter. Everyone else is the same.

Respect life. Respect all other people. Because each of us —all of us contributes to the greater whole of life. Everyone deserves respect.

Do Something Good Today
14/Apr/2020 09:08 AM

Do something good today. It doesn't have to be big or grand but remove yourself from your own melodrama for a moment, think about the bigger picture: the someone or the something else, and do something good.

Most people spend most of their time locked inside their own heads. They spend their time thinking about themselves: their wants, their needs, their cares, and their feelings. Take a moment and stop this process. Stop it and decide to do something good.

There is no absolute guidance as to what good you should do. But, we all know what good is based upon how we perceive bad. Good is helpful. Good is caring. Good is giving. Good is telling someone you love them. Good is thanking someone. Good is reaching out a hand of friendship. Good is good.

Take a moment, define good—define who or what you can do some good for and do it.

Do something good today.

*   *   *

14/Apr/2020 09:08 AM

The person who has done something bad to someone always wants to pretend that they did not do it.

* * *

13/Apr/2020 03:48 PM

What have you created lately?

No More Planes in the Sky
13/Apr/2020 12:02 PM

There are no more planes in the sky…

I guess, as the crow flies, I don't live that far from LAX. One way or the other, I would always look up and see planes flying through the sky. I'm not one of those people who would contemplate where they were going or anything like that, it was just something I would notice. Sometimes I would hear them before I saw them. Sometimes I would see them before I would hear them. Sometimes, particularly around sunset, I would watch their jet trials etch lines across the distant sky. Now, there are none. Literally, I look up and the sky is empty.

I was just outside on my patio listening to how quiet the world has become. No sound of car racing by on the nearby streets. Nobody talking. No sound of the jet engines in the sky. Very strange…

Since the dawning of the new age of reality brought about the coronavirus COVID-19 pandemic, life has changed. It has gotten so much quieter. I have heard that the air in L.A. is cleaner than it has been in generations. I remember going outside when I was kid, back before there were emission controls on the cars and all that kind of stuff, and my eyes would burn sometimes. It hasn't been that way for a long time, but smog is still very present in L.A. I guess, not now.

On TV you see things like monkey in herds taking over the streets in India and Thailand. I've encountered those little guys several times and they are crazy. I can imagine how scary it must be for the locals with those guys ruling the streets.

Life is different. Life is different for all of us. Life is different in different ways.

I'm sure life will get back to normal someday. There will be planes in the sky, a lot more smog, and less wildlife running wild in the streets. I guess that's good. That seems to be what everyone wants. But, it is bad too. Life has gotten so many quieter, especially for us urban dweller. So much more nature thriving everywhere.

I mean, think about it, how strange is the fact that there are no more planes in the sky?

The Blaming of Everyone
13/Apr/2020 11:15 AM

While listening to the news do you ever notice how many of the people in the public eye spend their time blaming others for the conditions that surround their life? This is particularly the case in politics. Everyone is blaming the other person or the other political party for the conditions of life.

Certainly, this spreads outwards to families. Think about how many children blame their parents for where they find themselves in life.

Move forward to relationships, and blame is immense. It seems everyone wants to blame someone else.

How about you? Think about your life. Who do you blame for what? But, more importantly, why do you blame them?

In politics, it is almost like a game. The game of reelection. Politicians need to run an election or reelection campaign to get a job and then keep a job. Some are very good at it. They have had their jobs for decades. But, how does one do that? They do that by criticizing, attacking, and/or blaming the other candidate. What do they blame them for? The answer, everything they don't like.

This is the same for the people that make up the various political parties. They support those of their party and they blame those of the other party. Wars have been fought over blame.

Religion… There has been more trauma and death instigated by religion than any other one element in human history. Yet, look at the religious teachers. They embrace their religion, they propagate their religion, and they blame others for the damage done to their religion by other people.

In personal relationships, blame is perhaps a bit more compartmentalized. This is especially the case within family dynamics. Many children blame their parents for causing them to have a defective childhood—for encountering childhood trauma or childhood unhappiness. They also blame them for unleashing poor psychological schooling which caused them to do bad things as they passed through their life. As true as all this may be, no matter the cause, as long as blame is used as the primary tool of interpersonal life-definition, all that is created is a life defined by blame.

Chosen personal relationships are also a sourcepoint for blame. People enter into a relationship via love, desire, or the hopes of life-betterment for any number of reasons. But, if that relationship does not provide all that is hoped for and one or both of the participants are left in a position of anger, loss, or unhappiness, oftentimes this culminates in blame.

But really, what is blame? And, how does blame come to define a person's life?

There are people who deliberately set about on a path to hurt the life of someone else. Those people are the lowest of the low. Most people aren't like that, however. Yes, there are people who should never be parents. Yes, there are people who should never be in relationships. Yes, there are people who should never be trusted. But, most people aren't like that. And, if a person operates from a perspective of consciousness, they stop themselves from doing the things that they would not be good at. This being said, so many people are cast into so many things that they have no control over; i.e.: who is a part of their family or that they are forced to do something like get a job that they do not like, that this lends one to either embracing life from a state of actualized transcendence or from encountering life based upon a state of blame defined by their feelings of unhappiness and remorse. But blame, always keeps an individual from entering into a more conscious understanding of life reality. Thus, it is a very poor choice of life definition.

In life, we are all dealt the card we are dealt. We do what we can from where we find ourselves.

In life, we all make choices. Most of these choices are based on our individualized desire. We want. We try to get. But, if we get, and then we are unhappy with what we got, who is at fault? Is it the fault of the what or the who we got? Or, is it our fault for possessing the desire for that something in the first place?

There is not much you can do about the family you are born into. There is not much you can do about the race or the culture you are born into. There is not much you can do, at least as a child, about where you find yourself in the socioeconomic strata. But, no matter where you find yourself, you can choose to own your now. You can choose to not try to place the blame elsewhere as a means of not taking responsibility for how you are feeling and what you are doing.

Life comes at all of us. We can only control it to the level we can control it. If we make a choice, we are responsible for that choice. No matter how badly that choice turns out. We are at fault. …Not anyone else involved. Stop the blame!

We each are dealt our family and our life situation. We may hate it. We may hate them. But, no matter what they do/what they did to us, it is we who can choose to transcend their limitations, never make the mistakes that they made, and rise ourselves to a new level of betterment. You may hate 'em but don't blame 'em, just realize what a low level creature they truly are, forgive them for not being whole enough to understand their own limitations, and make yourself more by not allow them to stop your growth by clogging your mind with blame.

*   *   *

13/Apr/2020 09:47 AM

One thing in life is certain; when you die, when you get to the other side of death, it is not going to be anything like you expected.

* * *

12/Apr/2020 03:06 PM

How many positive things do you do for other people, never take credit for, and they never knew you did them?

How many negative things have you said or done to someone else that they never knew you did?

* * *

11/Apr/2020 01:10 PM

To understand what someone is actually attempting to communicate you must have a mind developed to the degree that you can comprehend what they are presenting.

Why?
11/Apr/2020 08:00 AM

Why?

The question of, *"Why,"* is one of the most probing, perplexing, and penetrating questions a person can be asked. The reason this is such an explorative question is that most people do not have a clear answer for, *"Why,"* they do what they do. They don't think deeply about their actions. They just get an idea or are driven to an action by someone else. Then, they just do. But, the question of, *"Why,"* never enters their mind.

Think about your own life. Think about the things that you have done. Think about the big things and also thing about the small things. Why did you do what you have done?

For example, look at one of your life events that was very big. Something that changed your trajectory forever. Why did you do it? Look back though time and see how that event changed your life forever. Now, look back farther and think to the time before you took that action. Were you considering, *"Why,"* you were about to take that action or did it just happen?

Now, look to a small thing. Some seemingly inconsequential event in your life. This can be long ago or it can be yesterday. Why did you do it? Did you think about why you were about to do it or did you just do it? What affect did your doing it have on your life and perhaps more importantly what affect did your doing it have on the life of someone else?

This is one of the most important points to keep in mind. Your doing—the, *"Why,"* of your doing, not only affects your life but it has the potential to affect the life of everyone your doing may impact, now or in the future. With this, your karmic destiny is set into motion. So, the, *"Why,"* of your everything is essential to know.

Most people never think about their reason for, *"Why."* At

best, they will fill their mind with the, *"What they want."* Though desire is one of the most common causation factors for, *"Why,"* it is a very limited, selfish perspective.

Take a moment right now and contemplate the, *"Why,"* of where you find yourself in your life. Why are you where you are? Why are you feeling what you are feeling? Why are you living what you are living? Why are thinking what you are thinking? Why are you wanting what you are wanting?

Now, think about how your, *"Whys,"* of the past have affected your life of today. How have they led you to where you are now? How have they affected the life of others in both a positive and negative fashion?

The questioning of, *"Why,"* is one of the most penetrating and self-revelatory meditative practices that anyone can put into practice. Not only will it give you a better perspective of YOU it will provide you with a clearer pathway through life—one where everything just isn't caused by happenstance but it will provide you with a life defined by a clearer sense of true purpose—one where you can own your actions instead of living in a space of denial but you know, *"Why,"* you have done what you have done.

* * *

10/Apr/2020 10:56 AM

If you don't take anything from anybody then you don't owe anybody anything.

If you take something from someone then you owe them forever.

The Writer Verses the Reader
10/Apr/2020 09:45 AM

When you pick up a book, why did you decide to read it? Do you ever question this before you begin the read?

Commonly, you pick it up because you have an interest in the subject matter or it has been suggested to you. Though this is certainly the most common motivation for beginning to read a book, there is a completely different level of choice that comes into play in this matter. A level of choice that few people ever contemplate. That level of choice is formed by an individual's foundation of previously gained knowledge—how much someone thinks that they know about a particular subject.

Some people pick up a book loving the author, just because they are who they are. Other people pick up a book hoping to hate it. Very few, however, pick up a book holding a blank slate in the depths of their perception, nor do most people possess the ability to read a book and to truly accept it for what it is with no judgment.

To being to comprehend this subject a bit deeper let's initially look at it from the perspective of the author. Why does an author write a book? For the novelist, this calling is probably most pronounced as a means of creativity. They believe they have a story to tell and they tell it. For the nonfiction author, they are hoping to portray some understating that they have gained and desire to present it to others. With this as a basis, fictional and scholarly works have been composed throughout time.

The writer composes from a mindset of inspiration. This inspiration may come from any number of sources, but it is a unique and self-created discipline, internally developed that causes any individual to compose. No one can deny that creation is one of the higher forms of human consciousness as this is what defines human achievement and social understanding at any given point in history.

Now, ask yourself, what does the reader provide to this equation? Yes, they are the audience: they may like and/or they may learn from what they are reading but if they do not utilizes that knowledge and guide themselves towards a deeper understanding of life and human reality then what has reading that book truly proven?

Here arises the problem with the critical reader. They enter into reading a book from a previously defined state of mind. They go into reading a book believing that they already possess a deep basis of knowledge about what is being presented—and this goes to both literary and educational works. They go into the reading with the intention of voicing what they think or feel about the book, even if this is only in their own mind.

Think about when you read a book, what mental conversation is going on in your mind? Are you simply in a space of judgment-free knowledge acquisition or are you debating what is on the written page; what you like about it and what you don't?

How does the mental conversation of the reader contribute to the creative process? Is the reader the one who possessed the inspiration to write the book? Did they hold the creative vision? Did they have the skillset to present the fictional or the factional knowledge onto a page? The answer to these question is universally, no. They do not possess the foundational understanding or the internal motivation to create. Thus, what does their judgment of the work, whether it is in their own mind or verbalized to others, actually mean?

Most people, by the time the reach adulthood, no longer read books. Very few ever posses the desire or the ability to write a book. Yet, for those who do read, we return to the question presented at the beginning of this discourse, why are they reading the book in the first place?

In life, we all like what we like and we dislike what we dislike. That is human nature. But, how many people ever question, and seek to their depth of their subconscious mind, why they like what they like and why they dislike what they dislike? Why they think or verbalize what they like and why the think or verbalize what they dislike? And, more importantly, how many question why they feel the way they feel about a creative product, what is the source of their judgement, and what gives them the foundational righteousness to voice that judgment in the first place?

There is a certain group of people who base their entire life upon judgment. This may be actualized in a very subtle manner or it may become very vocal. But, does the critic ever take the time to know who they truly are and why they are expounding what they are claiming? Almost universally, the answer to this question is, no.

When you listen to a critic do you immediately believe what they are claiming? If you do, that mean you have relinquished your own sense of self-awareness and your own ability to explore the levels of your own human consciousness to that critic. Is that a pathway to self-realization?

Few people take the time to question their definition of consciousness. Few people possess the ability to study why they do what they do. Few people possess the ability to change, to expand, to explore, and to realize new levels of awareness within their life reality. How about you? Why do you read a book? How and why do you judge what you have read? And, why are you doing any of this in the first place? Think about it…

Are You Becoming Any Better?
09/Apr/2020 01:36 PM

Through each life event, the conscious individual strives to learn and become a better person. Yes, there are those who never change—those who never evolve or become the better representation of themselves. But, most of us are not like that. We want to be better. And, we understand to become better we must learn, change, and evolve.

In some ways we are blessed to be living when we are living in this Now. We are blessed because we are observing and living through the first global pandemic. Certainly, there have been other situations that have affected the entire globe but never one like this; the first global sickness that has pretty much brought much of the world to a halt.

What have you learned from this? How has it caused you to change your behavior? How has it caused you to become a better person? Or, have you not changed at all?

In each life event, large or small, we are presented with the opportunity to become a better representation of ourselves. If we look, if we listen, if we learn, we can truly become better through each life event.

How much time do you spend trying to learn? How much time do you spend trying to become better? How much time do you spend caring about others? How much time do you spend trying to help others? The answer to each of these questions will provide you with a clearer perspective of who you truly are.

Who are you? What are you? Do you only think about yourself? Or, do you think about others, putting them in front of your desires? If not, why not?

How have you changed from this pandemic? Are you one of the people hoarding the food and supplies that other people need? Are you one of the people taking? Or, are you one of the people giving?

Much of all of our lives goes by without too much of a thought. We do what we always do. But, every now and then something forces us to change our patterns—something forces us to change how we act, how we behave towards others, and what we do with and for others.

Have you taken note of how this pandemic has changed you? Have you taken note of the behavioral changes in you? If not, this is the time to do it. Take a look at you. Take a look at how you are doing what you are doing and why you are doing what you are doing. Take a look at what led you to where you now are in life and how that, *"Where you are,"* is affecting your behavior and your everything else in this Now reality.

Can you become better? Can you be more? Can you do more? Can you care more about others? Are you willing to care more about others?

What you are doing right now will set the stage for the rest of your life. What are you going to do right now? Are you going to think about yourself or are you going to think about others?

Life evolution begins with you. Let it begin now. Let it make you a better person.

What is Research?
07/Apr/2020 01:35 PM

What is research? It is finding out what you can about what has previously taken place. Research is not about founding a new method of anything. That is creation. Research is about exploring information that has been previously composed and presented, following that information to its source, and then concluding what you can by studying all that is available about a specific subject.

Most people doing research do not peer deeply into available materials. They do not do this because they do not possess the various skills necessary to reveal the truth. They do not hold the language skills or the ability to travel to the sourcepoint of where whatever available evidence originated. They are happy to simply listen to or read widely available communications.

The problem with this incomplete research is, however, a person is only presented with a limited set of facts commonly acquired and dissertated by one individual. Thus, most people are only reciting what someone else has previously said or has written. This is not research at all. It is simply expounding previously acquired communications from a person or persons that the information acquiring individual finds appealing.

People, through their own individualized process of indoctrination, develop a sense of belief. Belief is one of the worst culprits in the process of research because belief is not based in fact, it is simply based in conviction. Previously held beliefs keep one from penetrating the truth as they are locked into a stagnate mindset. In fact, some researchers only seek out verification for what they already believe. This is not research at all. This is simply false factualization.

To do research one must be willing to change their mind. This is what keeps most people from ever doing expansive research in the first place; their unwillingness to change their mind and to be open to new and different understandings that may differ from what they already believe.

There are some people who actually attempt to do true research. Because of the fact they are titled a, *"Researcher."* From this delineation they are often times given carte blanche credibility. This assumed trustworthiness can be bad, however, for some use this as a means to not have their research questioned. A true researcher forever seeks the truth even when this truth reveals that they may, at one point, have been wrong. On the other hand, there are those researchers who choose to fight for their point to become accepted reality instead of acknowledging the fact that no research is absolutely perfect and without fault.

Though each researcher, who does attempt to pierce the veil of understanding and take it to the sourcepoint of truth, can be commended, research is an ongoing process and, therefore, it is a never-ending activity of removing the guise of false understanding. Thus, research is forever on going. Research is never complete.

Each researcher contributes to the ever-growing and ongoing understand of the subject on which they focus. Some researchers claim, however, that the research ends with them. Some claim that they are right and that is that. To do this, however, attempts to end any further exploration driven towards the sourcepoint of the knowledge. Thus, claiming final and complete knowledge on any subject is vain and counterproductive to the overall expansion of human comprehension.

As each researcher progresses down his or her pathway new knowledge is revealed and new understandings are presented. From each researcher comes a unique level of observed realizations. Thus, the research of one researcher may be beneficial, it may even open up new doors of comprehension, but research never ends with one researcher. Research is ever ongoing.

Monday Night Class
07/Apr/2020 12:25 PM

There was a spiritual teacher named Stephen Gaskin, most commonly known as simply, *"Stephen."* He reached his height of popularity in the late 1960s and 1970s. Based out of San Francisco, he blended Eastern and Western Spirituality in association with Hippie Drug Culture. *The Grateful Dead* even did a song about him, *"Saint Stephen."* He was a strong force in that era but as time went on, like so many other teachers of times gone past, he has all but been forgotten.

Stephen was an interesting case study. He did his time in the Marines and then came to San Francisco where he earned a Master's Degree and taught at San Francisco State University for a time before changing life direction in association with the 1960s Cultural Revolution. He taught spirituality in San Francisco for a time and then moved his flock to a farm in Tennessee. Again, *The Grateful Dead* did a song about Stephen and his, *"Caravan,"* titled, *"Tennessee."* There, he was arrested for weed, did some time in prison, and reemerged onto the world stage.

I was lucky enough to meet and speak with him a few times. In fact, in my later teen years I pondered moving down to, *"The Farm,"* as it was titled. But, to do so would have meant I would have had to donate my car to the greater whole and I felt that was a bit much to ask in case I decided to leave.

All this being said, there were a few book published about the teachings and the lifestyle of Stephen. *"The Caravan,"* details his move to Tennessee. But, the first book published was titled, *"Monday Night Class."* This was based on the talks he would give each Monday night in San Francisco. All the, *"Stephen,"* books are all really good and if you are from a different generation or possessed a different mindset back then or just want a unique case study of the time they all make for a great read.

As you may know, I'm a bit of a bibliophile. I collect books. The problem is, I have a tendency to periodically give things away. This is the case with the hardcover edition of *Monday Night Class* I once possessed. I'm not quite sure when I gave it away or to whom but I no longer have it. Thus, for the past decade or so I have been trying to obtain a copy. They are rare and, as such, this has proven very hard to do. Every now and then I will see one advertised on Amazon, or some place like that, and I will buy it. Inevitably, I get them and it is not a hardcover copy at all but it is a softcover copy. This, even though I always contact the seller before buying it to confirm with them that it is, in fact, a hardcover. They always promise it is. But, that has never been the case.

This just happened to me again today. I ordered a copy that was described as a former library book. I contacted them and they promised it was a hardcover. I get it, and it is not.

It is not or was not intentional but I have started somewhat of a collection of all the softcover copies of *Monday Night Class* that I have received. I just stuck this newest/next copy on the shelf with the others. I now have seven. Combine those with the other copies I have donated to my local library and I have gone through this process more than a few times. Sure, they all have the same information in them. Some are in better condition that others. But, they are not what I ordered or was promised; i.e.: a hardcover edition.

You know, I am sure there is some deep spiritual lesson that could be learned from all this. And, I suppose, I could make one up. But mostly, all this just seems like it is an ideal example of life; the way some people encounter life, and the way some people behave towards others in life. For me, I always truthfully tell people what I have and what I have to offer. Many, however, don't care as long as they can possibly make a buck via misrepresentation.

There's a lesson in all this, I guess... But, I sure wish

someone would just send me what they claim they are offering and that I have purchased from them. Is it so much to ask for, a hardcover copy of, *Monday Night Class?*

*   *   *

07/Apr/2020 07:50 AM

How much of what you are given do you give back?

* * *
07/Apr/2020 07:50 AM

Small things equal large things.

* * *

06/Apr/2020 10:59 AM

How would that make you feel?

That is the question you need to ask yourself before you ever do anything to anybody.

* * *
06/Apr/2020 10:58 AM

How much of what you think and say is simply your projection of your own interpretation of what someone else actually created?

* * *

04/Apr/2020 07:17 AM

If all you are doing is proclaiming who you like verses who you don't like—who you believe is right verses who you believe is wrong you are doing nothing more than demonstrating to the world the limited spectrum of your perception.

* * *
04/Apr/2020 07:16 AM

If you spend your life focusing on all of the things that don't really matter at the end of your days you will have achieved nothing that actually did matter.

* * *

03/Apr/2020 05:25 PM

If you don't do it now you're going to have to do it later but with later comes all of the unknown variables.

The Conscious Moment
02/Apr/2020 09:11 AM

How much of your time do you spend living from a place of consciousness? How much of your time do you spend truly experiencing your moment? How much of your time are you very aware of what you are doing and very consciously engaged in what you are experiencing, whom you are experiencing it with, and why you are doing it in the first place?

The majority of life's people spend their life doing. They do but they never think about why they are doing what they are doing. If you ask them, they may give you a reason like this is their job or that is what they like to do but the interpersonal exploration of their, *"Why,"* never goes any deeper than that. They just do. But, they do not truly know why they do.

For most, each moment of their life is simply lived. They may be experiencing a sense of happiness or unhappiness engulfed in their moment but emotions are only sensation driven experiences, they are not realizations.

Think about your moment(s). Think about what you are living right now. Yes, you may be reading this but what are you truly experiencing? How in tune are you with what is going on around you? How experiential is your moment? Are you here in this now or is your mind thinking about something else?

This style of behavior is also very common with people interacting with other people. Yes, two or more people may be in a common space but how often are those two or more people truly encountering and experiencing one another? For the most part, people when they are in the presence of other people are simply thinking about something else. They are not truly intermingling their consciousness's in any absolute manner.

Why is this? Mostly, it is based in the way people are taught to encounter reality. They are trained to accept, to strive for, to accomplish, to dominate, to win, and to succeed. They are also taught that they should be happy. Thus, they are constantly seeking a means to make themselves happy. Though this is the training that most people undergo, this is also what keeps people from consciously embracing their moment.

Try this… Right now, experience your moment. Where are you? What do you hear? What do you see? What do your feel? How do you feel what you are feeling? How is what you are doing affecting the all and the everything around you? How is it affecting you? Truly feel and embrace your responses to those questions.

Next time you are with a person, truly experience that moment. If someone is close to you right now, go to them and truly experience the interaction. Feel what being in the presence of them truly feels like.

The only way you can ever truly come into a state of experiential consciousness is to embrace experiential consciousness. You must make the choice to consciously come into contact with what you are living and who you are living it with. It is only you who can do this.

Right now feel. Every time you are everywhere feel. Experience what and who you are encountering. Move into your moment and the true reality of all life will open up for you.

Consciously experience your every moment.

The World Under Lock Down
01/Apr/2020 08:29 AM

How much time do you normally spend at home? How much time do you spend embracing the nothing? How much time do you not try to achieve anything? How much time can you sit in your own silence?

For most people, they spend their entire life doing. They go to school until they go to work. They play. They watch TV. They listen to music. The readers read. The artists paint, write, play music, or create poetry. The actors act and the sewers sew. For most, all life is about the doing.

There are some who choose to find the silence in their being via meditation. But, those people are very few. The fact of the matter is, and as I have always said, for most, meditation is about the doing. They are doing something. They are meditating. Thus, even those who are walking on the spiritual path commonly never come to understand the true essence of meditation. For them, meditation is doing. But, that is not what true meditation is all about. Meditation is about the undoing.

During this pandemic, the world has attempted a forced shut down. People are supposed to stay home. Lock down. This is all new to the average person. Most have never been forced to do nothing.

So, there they are. There you are. You are home, (maybe alone), what are your supposed to do in your forced seclusion?

In my life, I've encountered a few lock down situations. The first was the L.A. Riots of '65. I lived in the hood back then. My father went off to his restaurant each day to keep it from getting looted while my mother and I stayed home. I would sit at our front window watching the National Guard troop carriers, tanks, and stuff, driving down our street. I saw soldiers carrying their rifles around their neck combing the neighbor. It was pretty intense.

The next time was in '71 with the big earthquake. Living in L.A. I had certainly felt earthquakes before but that one was pretty big. My mother behaved like noting had happened, got dressed and took the bus to work like always. The schools were closed so I sit there on the stoop of our apartment in Koreatown listing to KHJ AM rock radio and being pretty scared with each aftershock.

In each of those situations, I was doing. If nothing else, I was experiencing. But, this current situation is different in that we need to choose to stay in or risk getting something that may kill us. It's weird... Very-very weird...

You see on the news and the various other shows where people are talking about methods to keep the kids (and the adults) occupied in these times of coronavirus. All they discuss is what to do and new inventive methods to do it. That's all fine and great but why does no one try to not do? Why can't people let go? Why can't anyone sit in silence? Why does every moment of everyone's life have to be about doing?

For most of us, we grew up in the world of TV. We watched TV most of our lives. That is doing something. When we are driving we are listening to the radio, music, or podcasts. All this is doing. Speaking of my mother, she was a master seamstress. She just did it for fun. She also made some great stuff with crochet. She was always making something. My lady makes jewelry. Me, I used to play guitar for hours and hours on end. All that was doing. I have known some people who have made an art form out of getting drunk. For them, that is what they do. Pretty much everyone you know possesses his or her own style of doing, as do you. Tell me, do you know one person who can sit in his or her own silence and do nothing?

It has always been taught that life is all about the doing—it is about the accomplishing, it is about living the experience of the doing. But, is that all life is truly about? Is there not another, deeper, more refined realm where a person may be able to reach into their inner being and find a deeper understanding of Self, the universe, and maybe even god? But, to do that, you have to do nothing. You have to be silent. And, just like everything else and all the doing in life, becoming silent takes practice.

So, here we are. We are all told to shelter in place. We are asked to stay home. Most seek to fill their need for doing in this time when we are all asked to do nothing. There is another alternative, however. Instead of always finding something to do why don't you just take a moment in this time of abyss and embrace the abyss—encounter the silence. Let go of all that you are expected to do. Let go of all that you want to do. Let go of all of the faux doing you are attempting to create for yourself. This is the perfect time to encounter a new life reality. Stop doing and just Be. Try it. It may open up an entirely new level of conscious reality for you.

* * *

01/Apr/2020 07:24 AM

How many good things do you have to do to repair one bad thing that you did?

* * *

01/Apr/2020 07:01 AM

If enough people believe a lie does it become the truth?

* * *
01/Apr/2020 07:01 AM

When there is no right or wrong answer all you are left with is a choice.

*   *   *

01/Apr/2020 07:00 AM

If you practice at doing any technique incorrectly for long enough you get very good at doing something wrong.

* * *

31/Mar/2020 08:07 AM

Do you ever think about the person you could have helped but you did not?

Deflection for an Entirely Different Reason
31/Mar/2020 08:04 AM

As a martial artist, throughout the years, I have concentrated my primary focus on the art of deflection. Though my hard style training has certainly trained me in the forceful attack, I have always felt that the deflection of energy is a far better tool of self-defense than a blow-by-blow competition.

For anyone who has trained in the fighting arts or has been a keen observer, you will understand that the one powerful strike, to a venerable target spot on an opponent, will quickly put them down. This being acknowledged, there are so many reasons why not to do that.

As children and adolescences it is not uncommon that, particularly young boys, will punch it out. Witnessing one of those fights on the schoolyard, or remembering the ones that you might have had in your youth, are an ideal example of the wild randomness of street combat where fists are flying in all directions with little exact targeting involved.

As advanced fighting art training has become much more available in the recent decades, there have been many who have turned to formal martial arts instruction to gain a new, better, and more refined understanding of self-defense. With this has arisen a new breed of street combatant who is (perhaps) a bit more educated in their approach to physical combat. Though random flaying fists are still the most common name of the game in a street fight, there are those who have obtained training and have emerged feeling superior to the untrained opponent.

Certainly, formalized boxing has been around forever. And, the practitioners trained in this fighting art are some of the most proficient in rapid, hard style, self-defense. There is a problem in all forms of hard style self-defense, however, and that problem is cultural definition.

As a child or adolescent, if you punched it out, you

punched it out. Somebody won, somebody lost, or the bout was broken up and you moved on. Maybe you even became friends soon after that. In adult life, it is not like that, however. If you punch somebody, and even if they punched you first, if you defeat them, they are probably going to call the cops, you are probably going to get arrested, and then they will probably sue you. Sure, you kicked their ass. Sure, the charge may not stick. Sure, you may counter sue and you may even win the lawsuit, but all of that will cost you a lot of time, a lot of money, and a lot of frustration. But, what if you didn't punch them at all. What if you did nothing but defend yourself in a non-aggressive manner? Who could they sue?

Certainly, walk away from any physical confrontation that you can. They are just stupid! But, if you are being attacked, you do not have to punch or kick an opponent to win the confrontation.

Now, I am not trying to sell a specific style of martial arts here or anything like that. I am not trying to say that one style of fighting art is better than another. What I am saying is that if you can learn the techniques to deflect a physical attack and if you allow your attacker to charge at you and you then simply redirect their energy in a manner that will cause them to be injured to the degree that the confrontation will stop with throwing a punch, you walk away free of fault.

In my life, even in my adult years, there have been people that have grab or rushed at me. I always warn them first but if they continue forward with their attack then I have, at least initially, applied deflective self-defense.

The good news about getting older, at least from my perspective, is that there are less people that want to attack you. You are generally not in situations, like rowdy bars, where some drunken fool, fueled by liquor, wants to fight. What's the fun and where's the honor in fighting an old guy? But, that's just me. For you, there may come a time when you have to defend yourself.

And, for this, you need training.

Most forms of traditional martial arts take a lot of time until you get to the level where you can effectively defend yourself with the techniques taught within each system of self-defense. Boxing, on the other hand, gets the student training in effective fighting techniques almost immediately. Though, as detailed, the techniques taught in boxing lend to the entire problem discussed with defending yourself in a forceful manner.

Whenever I teach seminars on the fighting arts, almost universally I train the students in the art of elemental deflection. Whether they are a long-trained martial artist or a novice, I teach them simple, doable methods of getting out of the way of the attack and then possibly using the attacker's own energy against themselves. All this does not have to be hard or complicated. The easiest way to accomplish this is to just step aside. A guy is throwing a punch with a right hand, quickly step to your right and the punch will miss you.

Training in what to do next is a bit more complicated and it can't be described in just a few words on this page. But, you get the point. Get out of the way of an attack. Once this has happened, you didn't get hit, you didn't punch anyone, and a whole new world of reality and opportunity opens up for you.

This is the same with life. There are aggressive, confrontational people out there. People that want to fight. People that like to fight. People who have trained to fight so they believe that they hold the advantage, which is the only reason they want to fight in the first place. We can all agree that those are not nice people. They are not highly evolved people. But, they are out there, nonetheless. What do you do when you encounter someone like that? Don't fight, simply sidestep the attack. Then, just walk away.

This is the ideal tool in both physical and verbal confrontation. Walk away first, that's the best defense. Never attack. But, if they attack, move out of the way of the attack. Let them expend their own energy while you do nothing but step to the side and walk away.

Kung Flu Zombies
AKA A Bunch of Neighbors I Don't Want To Know
30/Mar/2020 10:01 AM

The world has pretty much shut down. It is really kind of crazy, don't you think? A month ago did you anticipate that there would be no toilet paper on the shelves in the supermarkets because everyone is hoarding it? …Lines to get in the supermarkets when before there were none.

If we look across the globe, there are many cultures and societies that are forever struggling. But, in the free world, I never saw this coming. Did you?

The world shut down all due to unsanitary, unhealthy condition in a market in China. From there, the disease spread outwards, embracing the entire globe, and there is nothing that anyone can really do about it. So many people have gotten sick and have died and the numbers are rising. Thanks China!

Here in L.A., there is this massive stay at home suggestion. As this is America, (land of the free and home of the brave), and people have freedom and rights, there is really nothing anyone can do to stop anyone from doing anything, and there are always the arrogant, the selfish, and the rebellious who do whatever the fuck they want. But, that is not good in this situation where the transmission of this disease is from person to person.

Once the stay at home suggestion went into effect and all of the churches, gyms, restaurants, and shopping malls were closed, many of the people, who are currently not working because where they worked has been shut down, decided to see this as a vacation so they took to the beaches, the trails, and the parks. Then, the cities and countries shut all of them down, as well. Closed signs are everywhere. But, it is suggested that people still get outside and get some exercise as long as they do the social distancing thing. But, that's hard to establish on the sidewalks of a city like L.A.

Yesterday, I was doing some cardio walking at this secret location I know of, where no one goes, but as I was walking home, into my neighbor, it was like a fucking zombie apocalypse, all these people walking around—people who never walk. The sidewalks were full of people: blank eyed, not knowing where to go or what to do. Some pushed baby carriages, some had a dog on a leash, and some were just randomly wandering. It was really a scary sight. Like the song from the '80s proclaims, *"Nobody walks in L.A."* Yet, all these people were walking on a crowded suburban sidewalk, no one was keeping the social distancing guidelines. Walking on a street that you rarely ever see anyone walking on, unless they are walking to their car.

I don't know what's going to happen from all of this. I don't know where it will end. But, the world is currently shut down, at least all of the, *"Out there,"* is closed.

People adapt. But, have you ever noticed that the people who walk out the other side of a cataclysmic event are always the ones who went into with a solid foundation and basis of substance and/or those who are willing to walk all over anybody, do whatever it takes, to get what they need and want? Which of those do your believe is the best and the most karmically pure?

Me, I don't want to know any of the people walking down my street. I have no reason to know them. I'm sure, just like in every other situation of my life they would want something from me but offer me nothing in return. And, I guess that's the point. This life situation is crazy! None of us have any control over it as the all and the everything about it is out of our control. All we can be, in these life situations, (in all undesired life situations), is as conscious of behaving to the best of our ability with the cards we are deal.

There is no controlling this pandemic. Hopefully it will soon pass and it will only be a bad memory. But, this isn't the only bad thing that's going to happen in your life. *"Shit happens."* So, who are you? What is your foundation? Does your foundation provide you with a means and a method to get through this pandemic and other negative life events with a clear framework of focus and substance?

Who are you? What are you? Are you a taker, not caring about the anyone else, doing things like hoarding toilet paper so other people have none? Or, are you the person who is foundationally stable in your existence, in your occupation, in your faith, or in your life understanding, so much so that you may remain conscious, caring, self-contained, self-controlled, and giving?

When negative life events occur, it is what you do in those moments that sets the destiny for the rest of your life into motion. What are you doing?

Conspiracy Theory for the Day: Think about all of the protests that were going on in Hong Kong. They had been going on for months and the Chinese government couldn't do anything to stop them. They knew they couldn't do another Tiananmen Square as the eyes of the world were on them. Enter COVID-19 and the protests stopped.

* * *

29/Mar/2020 10:30 AM

Think about if every time you ate a piece of fruit you planted the seeds from that piece of fruit how much better the world would be.

Where Does Your Stuff Go When You Donate It?
28/Mar/2020 09:02 AM

I think for many of us, as we entered into the twenty-first century, and even before, we hope to help the world and those in need in any small way that we can. From this, as thrift stores have become a cultural norm, we donate our unused or used clothing, our electronics, our everything with the hopes that someone will be able to benefit from us moving those items along. But, have you ever pondered the questioned, *"Where does my stuff go once it is donated?"*

I remember back maybe twenty years ago now, there was a book store that I really liked going to. It was having a bit of hard go, so I donated a bunch of rare, printed in India, first edition, books from this one author to them in order that they could sell them and hopefully add to their coffers. Maybe two or three years later this man contacted me who had apparently purchased a large percentage of those books. He told me he had purchased them at the time they were first offered and he had just figured out how he could get in touch with me. The backstory is, I obtained those books back in a period of time when I had this, *"From the Library of Scott Shaw, Ph.D."* embosser and I would stamp the first page of all of the books in my library. Anyway, the guy went on and on about how spiritual he was and how that one author was a major influence in his life and made all things in his life and the world a whole lot better. Okay… Great! Then, he goes into this whole really negative discourse about how I was a total asshole in that I had ruined the books by stamping them with my name. My response, *"Why did you buy them then?"*

This is the thing about life; we all operate and do things from our own perspective. We do things as best as we can and we do them from where our minds are based at each point in our life's evolution. Some of us even try to help other people. We do what we do, but what we do may not be appreciated by others.

This also brings us to the whole concept of energy and energy transference. Many people, including myself, believe that objects possess an energy. …That certain objects, particularly when they are well-focused upon, hold onto that energy. How a person lives, what a person does where they live, and what they do with the items that surround their life, causes them to possess the energy of their existence. Thus, when you pass things along, they possess your energy and when you buy things, "Used," those items possess the energy of the person or persons who used them before you. This is why some people do not want to pass their used items along to others. This is also why some people do not want to buy used items.

So here we are in life… Not everyone has the same energy as we do. We may like the energy of some people—we may like what they do or do not do. Others may like our energy—they may like what we do or do not do. Just the opposite is true, as well.

Do you want the energy of someone else? Do you want to give someone else your energy? In the world of give and take all this can and should be considered. Or, like most, it may never be thought of at all. And, perhaps that is the best way to encounter life… …Never think about anything. Of course, from this mindset is born a lot of random senseless actions that may damage your life or the life of others. But, for those of us who care about others, those of us who think about the betterment and wellbeing of others, we must step beyond all stages of condemnation and energy manipulation. For if we are to care, if we are to give, we have to care more about the act of caring and the act of giving than what someone will think about our giving. We cared. We gave. We tried to make the all and the everything just a little bit better. Isn't that the ultimate definition of a life well lived?

* * *
28/Mar/2020 09:01 AM

You can only care about what you are going to eat when there is something to eat.

Because You May Never See It Again
27/Mar/2020 07:53 AM

This whole coronavirus COVID-19 pandemic has really changed the world forever. Just a month ago, for most people, everything was going along as normal. No more. Now, we are all confronted with the fact that at any moment our life may be taken away from us. With this knowledge, it is an ideal time to rethink the way in which you encounter your reality.

There is this street that overlooks a beach not far from where I live. It is a bit unique for the area in that it is a few hundred feet about the beach, so when you park and get out of your car you have a very wide spanning view of the sand, the ocean, and the bike path that goes along the coastline.

Whenever I am driving by, I stop there just to take a moment with the sea.

I have always loved the ocean. I guess being from Southern California that goes part and parcel will the local existence. Due to this, I spent many of my adult years living right next to the ocean. It was a choice. Though yeah, everything does gets rusty pretty quickly, there is just something about the meditative, hypnotic effect of the waves.

Many people don't like it. They find it noisy. There was many a girl I brought over, way back in the way back when, who couldn't sleep due to the ongoing sonic caress. Me, who is a notoriously light sleeper, does not have a problem with it, however. Anyway, I love the ocean.

There I stood yesterday, looking out over the ocean, taking in the sounds of the waves and the scenery. I noticed a social distancing sign and took a photo of it with the people in the background walking and biking way too close to each other—too close at least in term of the new rules and regulations. I posted it on my Instagram.

Then, I turned and went back to my car. I caught myself. *"Wait a minute. I may never see this again,"* I said to myself. I realized that I had really been out of my moment. I had a lot on my mind yesterday and though I was there, at this beautiful, spiritual location, my mind was elsewhere.

What I did was to walk back to the overlook and really take a moment and take it in. Experience it.

Here's the thing, we each have those places that are very special to us. Wherever we find ourselves in the world, we have a place—a place that even if we see it everyday, there is something that draws our mind back to it.

The truth of life is, there are no guarantees. There never has been. We can leave this place called life at anytime and we may never even see the exit coming. Here, today, admits this pandemic, we are simply constantly reminded of this fact.

The thing is, during this time in history, or any other time, you really need to consciously experience you moment. You really need to live your moment. You really need to appreciate your moment. So, when you are there, wherever you are, take the time to look, to see, to feel, and to experience that place because you may never see it again.

Instead of Hurting Why Don't You Lend a Helping Hand
26/Mar/2020 09:27 AM

In this modern world, it seems that there are so many people so full of their own all and everything deciding that they know what other people should or should not be doing. They believe they know what other people should or should not be thinking. They have all kinds of knowledge about other people and what they are doing wrong. They have a voice, (very loud sometimes), that screams at the top of their lungs, telling the world how wrong some other person is. They critique, they criticize, they diminish, and they hurt.

In this modern world, it seems that there are so many people so full of their own all and everything deciding to take some action that has the potential to hurt someone else. They feel they are justified in their actions. They feel they have a reason and a purpose. They feel they are right and that other person is wrong. Maybe they even find cohorts to help them carry out their plan. They devise it, they execute it, and then they watch as the castle crumbles. But, what does hurt ever truly equal in this world? What does destruction ever truly equal in this world? How does it make anything better to hurt someone else: their life, their work, their possessions, or their creations?

When we look out onto the world, when we look out onto life, most of the world's people live a very simple existence. They are not the one's reading this blog. They have no way to read to this blog. They are simply trying to survive.

It is the people with time on their hands that set about focusing their attentions and their intentions onto the life of other people. They do this because they are not in the trenches, struggling to survive, trying to put a roof over their head and food on the table for their family.

The people who hurt, the people who intentionally hurt, are the lowest form of human existence. Think about anyone who has hurt anybody, why did they do it? Did they do it for the good of the person they were hurting? Or, did they do it for themselves to gain something: money, power, ego, or an enhanced sense of self worth?

If you hurt you hurt. Does hurting ever help?

Now, let's turn this around and think about it from a different perspective. How many of the people who hurt others also take the time to help others? Do they devise a plan to make their community or the world a better place? In virtually all cases, the answer to that question is, no.

There are, however, people on the other side of this equation. There are people who set about on a course and devise plans that do not hurt anyone and actually do make the something of someone just a little bit better. Do these people do this for themselves and to make themselves feel good about themselves? Maybe. But, what they have created in devising a plan to help others and hurt no one overshadows any ego gratifications they may gain from actualizing a strategy of doing something kind, good, nice, and helpful.

So, what are you going to do today? Are you going to think about someone you don't like or disagree with? Are you going to talk about them and voice your disagreement? Or, are you going to make a decision to consciously refocus your mind and devise a plan to help someone, maybe even someone you disagree with.

Like I often discuss, your life is your choice. What you do with it is your choice. This is especially the case when you have the time to think about these things. This is especially the case when you have the time to do.

Everything becomes so much better when people step outside of their own judgments and lend a helping hand. You can do this anywhere, anytime. Right now, look around yourself; wherever your find yourself. Do something helpful. You are probably online right now. You can do it there. Wherever you are, do something nice. Do something good. Do something helpful. Reach out, and instead of hurting, why don't you lend a helping hand?

* * *
24/Mar/2020 05:57 PM

What have you done to save the world today?

A Good Time to Change
24/Mar/2020 05:43 PM

As we pass through this COVID-19 pandemic we are all being confronted with the realities of life. People are getting sick and people are dying all over the world. We are presented with their illnesses and the impact this pandemic is having on all aspects of life all across the globe every time we are On-line or turn on the TV or the Radio.

The numbers of those dying are staggering but most people do not care about this fact. They do not care because it is not them who has becoming deathly ill or has lost a loved one. For them, all that is off there in the distance. Most are just attempting to make sure that they have hoarded enough toilet paper.

I have watched as people who live in an area that is not yet highly impacted by this virus going on with their life with little thought about the wide spanning consequences of their actions. They are not sick, their family or friends are not sick, thus they believe that they can behave like everything is normal. But, everything is not normal. Nothing will ever be the same again. Like I have long said, everything you do has the potential to directly affect everyone else on this planet as the actions you unleash moves outwards from your instigation. And, if you do not care when you hurt someone/anyone there is really something wrong with you and you should investigate why you behave that way and stop it!

People are vain. People foolishly believe they can be stronger than a virus. People believe they can pray it away. But, think about it, I am sure many of the people who have passed away from COVID-19 thought they were strong and I would imagine that most of them were praying as they died.

With the factual reality of our lives changed forever, this is the ideal time to take a long hard look at your life and the wide spanning affects of your actions. This is a good time to change. Even if you are not being directly affected by this pandemic, the world around you is suffering and you should care about that fact because we all have played a part in where we find ourselves in this place in history.

Like I always say, the universe begins with you. What you do not only affect you, your life, and your karma but it spreads outwards to all those people you know and from there all the people they know and onwards and onwards. Thus, you are the sourcepoint of all reality. Accept your responsibility.

This is the time to help everyone that you can. This is the time to make everyone's life better that you can. Start with those you have hurt. Apologize and try to fix what you did to them. That's the hard one. That's the one that takes selflessness and a diminished ego. Then, go for the easy one, reach out a hand of embrace to those you like and those you love. Even if you don't (yet) physically know them, let them know that you appreciate their being a part of your life and tell them that you care about them. Embrace compassion. Look around you, if someone needs help, help them.

This world is hurting right now. Many people are hurting. Many people are dying. Do something about it! The world begins with you.

We can all change. We can all be better. We can all do things better. We can all do things that make a positive difference in the lives of other people. Allow this horrendous pandemic to cause you to change. Stop only thinking about yourself, your desires, and your needs. Stop hurting other people. Be more than that! Step outside of your mind and choose to care about others. Choose to do for others.

Everybody's life is important. When you realize that then you begin to think about how your actions affect other people and how your actions may bring about a positive change in all those you encounter.

Help this world. Help this world's people. Help us get through this pandemic.

The Lessons People Learn
23/Mar/2020 08:38 AM

It's kind of interesting, when I wrote a blog about this coronavirus COVID-19 pandemic a little while back I assumed that would be it on the subject. But, this whole thing has come to define so much of our lives that it has presented so many new realities and so many new life lessons that it is impossible not to think about.

For each of us, defined by where we live, we are now presented with a new, different, and unique reality. For some, it has not affected their life too much. For others, like those in Italy, their lives have been upended and so many innocent people have died. But, as the question is often posed, who is innocent?

Here in L.A., the city has been virtually shut down. There are a lot of people being told to not go to work, which has opened up a lot of free time that a lot of people did not previously possess. All this being said, there has been a six-foot rule applied in hopes of keeping people safe from contracting the virus. Sure, you can still exercise: go take a walk, a bike ride, a hike, etc., but you are supposed to stay six feet apart. But, no one listens. For example, over the weekend, the news crews showed people crowded, elbow-to-elbow, on the Malibu pier, thousands of people on the beaches, tons of people up at the L.A. Observatory. There were all these families sitting on the lawn up there happily interacting and smiling only a few inches away from one another. There were even these two guys doing a boxing workout on the lawn: one doing the gloves and other holding the focus mitts. At another location, there is this private, member's only, golf course that had hundreds of people out on the links and they told the news crews to get off the property. I mean, come on...

There is this trail not far from where I live that my lady and I periodically hike on. Normally, you will maybe see one other person or maybe a couple walking on it, if that. I predicated there was going to be more this past weakened but I could not believe my eyes when we were doing our walk. There were so many people on it. Some people were rudely not even trying to keep their distance from other people on the smaller, more confined, parts of the trail. Just claiming the trail as their own, not caring that they were walking very close or bumping into someone else.

I was in the supermarket on Sunday and I had kind of a weird experience. I was having a little bit of a problem with the self-checkout machine and the cashier came up to help. She came so close to me that I had one of those weird flashes of logic. She brought her face so close to my face that it felt like one of those times when you're on a first date and your face gets very close to your partners and you sit there in contemplative hesitation for a moment before you finally kiss.

This is kind of the exact opposite of what happened to me at the supermarket a few days before when the six-foot rule just went into effect. There were a lot of people there. Everybody is hoarding now. I was pushing my cart down the isle and I came up behind a woman. I guess when she turned around she was startled to see somebody there. But, I mean, there were a lot of people in the isle of that store. She, with a crazed look in her eyes, blurts out, *"Six feet! Six Feet! I want to stay six feet a part!"* Everybody but her smiled as she was behaving so much like a character in a low budget horror movie. She scurried away down the isle with her cart full of toilet paper.

A lot of people are getting sick. One of my friends apparently has contracted the virus. She had the high fever and the shortness of breath so she went to an urgent care facility. All they did was tell her to go home and self-quarantine. They didn't give her any meds. They didn't even test her, as they did not have a test kit to perform the test. First of all, she smokes. So, she too is at fault as she has placed herself in a position of respiratory vulnerability. And, all these mile long lines of cars you see on the news waiting for a test from their vehicle is not the reality on the ground. Plus, if a person does not have it today, they may contract it tomorrow. So, what good are the tests anyway unless you perform them on a daily basis? Moreover, and perhaps this is a conspiracy theory, but, do you think they are not compiling a record of your DNA when they perform these tests? I mean, they are getting a lot of people giving up the secret code to their life and existence with no questions asked.

There are a lot of life lessons that can be learned from all of this. A microscope has been provided, providing an enhanced method to peer into society and individual consciousness. I mean, simply look at the behavior of the greater masses and you can learn a lot about your society. Look at the way people behave— look at how you behave in this time of great toils and you may come to understand a lot about your life and life in general.

People are a selfish breed. Look at all the hoarding that is going on—people are only thinking about themselves and the people who are close to them. Doing this, while robbing others from the needed necessities of life.

People think only about themselves and doing what they want to do with the people they want to do it with. So, they congregate in individualized masses, putting so many at risk of contracting COVID-19 which can prove to be deadly. So, their actions are literally killing people.

How about you? What are you doing? What are you doing to keep you and your loved ones safe, healthy, and sane? How are you providing for them? How has this pandemic altered your reality and your life-consciousness, and how will you precede forward with your life if you survive?

I don't know what's going to happen. I don't know what's going to happen next. I hope you are all fine and will remain fine. But, you can get this potentially deadly disease simply by touching something someone has touched hours ago and then touching your face like we all so often do. That's why places like New York has been hit so hard. Think of the subways.

For anyone who reads this blog you know I generally don't quote the scripture very often but this whole thing just seems so biblical I cannot help myself. Forgive me...

Corinthians 6:14-18, *"Do not be unequally yoked with unbelievers. For what partnership has righteousness with lawlessness? Or what fellowship has light with darkness? What accord has Christ with Belial? Or what portion does a believer share with an unbeliever? What agreement has the temple of God with idols? For we are the temple of the living God; as God said, I will make my dwelling among them and walk among them, and I will be their God, and they shall be my people. Therefore go out from their midst, and be separate from them, says the Lord, and touch no unclean thing; then I will welcome you, and I will be a father to you, and you shall be sons and daughters to me, says the Lord Almighty."*

So You Have a Memory
22/Mar/2020 07:55 AM

For each of us we have memories of the things we have encountered in our lives. Some of these memories are very short lived. Yes, they are held somewhere in the annals of our brains but they are lived, thought of maybe once or twice and then never thought of again. Then, there are memories that are constantly remembered. Maybe they are found memories, maybe they are bad memories, but for whatever reason we remember those memories quite frequently.

Some memories we want other people to know about. We live an event, we remember an event, we want to tell others about that event. Other memories, we want no one to know anything about.

Some memories are created solo. We are the only one having lived the event that inspired the memory. Other memories are lived in association with another person or other people. Though they are lived with other people, it is us who is living them and it is us who is remembering them, and thus, they are uniquely interpreted in our own mind. How we experienced the experience may not be how the other person(s) involved in that event experienced that experience thus the experience may be remembered completely different by each individual.

For some, they like to discus the lives and the memories of other people. In my life I have had people attempt to detail my life events and my life memories to others. But, as that person is not me, as they did not actually experience the events, as they do not know what I was thinking, feeling, or why I was thinking, feeling, or why I was doing what I was doing they have been completely wrong in their interpretation and/or documentation of my lived memory. This is the same for all who attempt to detail the life memories of anyone.

Each person has their life memories, but what do life

memories actually equal? Sure, they mean something to the person who possesses the memories but what do they mean to anyone else? Do they mean anything to anyone else?

      Think about all of the people who have lived throughout time. They each had their own unique set of memories. They live, they died, they perhaps relayed their memories to a few other people but then they were gone, they died, their memories were erased. Some people, like me, put some of their memories to type. But, most do not. They simply live what they live, remember what they remember, until they remember it no more. So, what do memories actually equal? Think about that, what do memories actually equal? What do your memories actually equal?

Expressing it with Love. **Expressing it with Hate.**
21/Mar/2020 07:54 AM

"May you live in interesting times." Though tongue in cheek, this is a curse that is attributed to having originated in China. Though the actual source of this statement is not known, I think it ideally illustrates what we are going through today with the global pandemic COVID-19 having originated in China. Thus, the curse and the curse were both born in China.

No one can argue that this is a crazy time. The city of L.A. and all its surrounding communities are shut down. "Safer at home," they say. No one is going to work and the businesses are all closed. That's the same for San Francisco and its surrounding communities. New York is shutting down Sunday night. And, there are many other communities that are or will be doing the same thing. That's nuts!

I think back to just a couple of weeks ago. Though the COVID-19 was in the news, life was going on as normal.

Certainly, there are a lot of fingers that can be pointed as to who is to blame for this pandemic. And, as I have said in the past, why is no one taking China to task for letting this happen as this is not only going to kill people but it will financially ruin a lot of people's lives. Think if this pandemic arose from a country that we were at odds with. Or, if it had been knowingly unleashed it. There would be bombs flying through the air. Instead, all any one is doing is blaming while the world, literally, falls apart.

If you watch CNN all the anchors do is to throw shots at and blame the president; subtly or blatantly. Go to Fox News and they unleash praise. But, the fact of the matter is, no matter who was or is the president during this crisis, and whether you love him or hate him, nobody knows exactly how to handle this situation, because it has never happened before, and all any politician can do is to do the best that they can do and I believe that is what's happening. Do I believe everything everyone, in a position of power, is doing in regard to this situation is correct? No. But, I am a nobody. All I can do is play along.

If you look back through history, there were times when things like the bubonic plague or the Spanish Flu killed a lot of people. Complete civilizations, like the Mayans, were wiped out and we don't even know why. But, in those cases, the spread of the disease was relatively isolated. Now, COVID-19 is impacting the entire globe and who knows where all this will end and what will come in its aftermath.

You know, I used to think I would probably die by getting jacked in some back alley in Bangkok or some place like that. Back in '96, I was attacked by five assailants in Bangkok. But, I pretty readily defeated all of them. Then, I thought I would probably go out some day like my father from a massive heart attack. …Not yet anyway… But, who ever envisioned that all of these people would be dying from this unseen killer disease born in a Chinese marketplace because the people who inhabit that area eat, what we would consider, unsavory foods and offer those foods up in a very unsanitary manner? Sure, a lot of people die from the flu every year. But, *"The flu,"* was not introduced to us by some foreign power who doesn't choose to govern its people. Thus, all this pandemic occurred by a government making a choice. A choice to not keep their people clean. People are dying all across the globe due to a culture's uncleanliness.

Deuteronomy 28:59, *"Then the lord will bring upon you and your descendants extraordinary plagues—great and prolonged plagues—and serious and prolonged sicknesses."*

John Fogerty, *Creedence Clearwater Revival,* *"I hope you got your things together. I hope you are quite prepared to die. Look's like we're in for nasty weather. One eye is taken for an eye Don't go 'round tonight it's bound to take your life. There's a bad moon on the rise."*

People some how possess a belief that they are in control of their life. But, this is anything but true. Sure, most of most people's lives go along without too much radical change, but sooner or later loss, sadness, catastrophe, and/or death hits us all. This being said, it is all how we deal with each of these events in our life that defines how those events will define our life. Though we cannot control life, we, personally, do have the power to decide how we will behave.

How do you behave? Do you attack, criticize, say bad things, do bad things just because you don't like a person or do not agree with how they are interacting with their life and/or handling specific situations? Or, do you forever encounter the world in a positive, good-natured, caring, and understanding manner?

We each live our lives as best as we can. We each do what we do defined by external circumstances that we have no control over. All this being said, what we do, how we do it, and how we react to life events is all a choice that we can choose to make. Yes, some of us may get sick from this pandemic. Yes, some people may die. But, no matter what happens to us in our lives, by choice or by otherwise, we each have a choice about how we encounter that event. What are you going to do next?

* * *
21/Mar/2020 07:53 AM

Can you point to the place in your life where someone did something to you that changed the evolution of what you were compared to what you became?

Survival
18/Mar/2020 09:28 AM

There is this black and white cat that lives in the field below where I live. Once upon a time there was a whole colony of his black and white relatives. I watched one group of kittens grow to adulthood and give birth to the next generation. Now, they are all gone with only this one left. What happened to them? I have no idea. All I know is that they are gone. Somehow, this one cat is remaining. And, he (or she) looks healthy. He is a little chubby, maybe eating from the neighbor's dog food dishes or something. He has survived.

I have long been an aquarium enthusiast. From the time African Cichlids arrived in the U.S. in the 70s, I was a big fan. The only problem with that breed of fish is, they tend to be very aggressive towards one another. When they are young they all get along pretty well, as long as you provide them with the appropriate hiding spots. As times goes on, however, one fish generally turns out to be the bad ass and he eventually pretty much kills everyone else in the tank. Then, a new flock needs to be brought in.

Several years back, I discovered African Leaf Fish. They are from the same family as Cichlids but they are not near as aggressive. They pretty much live and let live. Toss in a couple of upside catfish and few other larger fish breeds and it is a fun aquarium.

When I was first found out about African Leaf Fish I had several Albino Cory Catfish patrolling the bottom of my aquarium. The African Leaf Fish were fine with them. They each were allowed to live their life. Time goes on, however, and Albion Cory's don't have that long of a life span. So eventually, they were all gone.

A couple of months ago I was in an aquarium shop and decided to buy a few more. I put them in the aquarium, thinking they would be fine. Each day, however, their numbers diminished. This continued until there was only one left. Who's been eating them? I don't know. But, all but one is gone.

Now, every now and then I see this one Cory sneaking out from behind the plants and the rock. He looks fine. Sadly, like the cat in the field below me, he is all alone. But, like the cat he has survived, he is a survivor.

Why do some people survive and even thrive when all others around them are gone? I don't know? Maybe it is their ability to be stealth and blend in. Not fight, not be obvious, but to find their place, find their niche, find a means of survival, and just live. Because, living is all any of us truly have. It is only when we are alive that we can feel, that we can do.

Most people try to be obvious. They want to be seen. Some are even willing to fight. They are willing to attack. They are willing to hurt. And, they don't care who they are hurting as long as they are not being hurt. But, this style of survival only leads to the kill or be killed mentality. And, if you live this style of survival, just as the saying goes, *"Live by the sword, die by the sword,"* which was derived from Matthew 26:52, *"Put your sword back in its place,"* Jesus said to him, *"For all who draw the sword will die by the sword."*

Life is complicated. It is complicated to find a conscious means of survival. It is hard to survive, especially if you are all alone and doing it on your own. But, by being silent in your truth, whatever your truth may be, you encounter no conflict and from this you may glide under the radar of those who will attack and find a happy life in your peaceful, meditative existence.

Kung Flu Rapture
17/Mar/2020 08:59 AM

Luke 17:34-36, *"I tell you, in that night there shall be two men in one bed; the one shall be taken, and the other shall be left. Two women will be grinding together: the one will be taken and the other left. Two men will be in the field: the one will be taken and the other left."*

The Christian concept of Rapture has been interpreted in different ways by different preachers and traditions throughout the centuries. There has even been a few movies made based on this concept. This being the case, the commonly accepted understanding about Rapture is that the holy, the good, and the faithful will immediately be taken up to heaven while the others, the not so pure and holy, will remain on earth for a time at the time of Revelations when Jesus will return to earth.

With this whole coronavirus COVID-19 thing going on, and the movement and activities of people being limited by local governments, that whole concept is kind of illustrative of today's world. There are those, the unholy, who are willing to take to the streets to do whatever it is they feel like doing and then there are those, the holy, who stay in their homes in seclusion.

I was in one of the restaurants I frequent yesterday. Now, in L.A., all of the restaurants have been forced to close by the government except for takeout or delivery. As I live in one of the surrounding city, the edicts of the L.A. mayor did not travel to my community as least not as of yesterday—today it has gone county wide. Anyway, I was going in there at lunchtime when normally it is overrun with people. Yesterday, there was like one solo person, a young couple freed from their high school obligations due to the fact that their school has been closed and one other couple. When I walked in with my lady, I was closely followed by this elderly man who quickly exclaimed you can sit anywhere you want. Sometimes, when it is not crowded in this restaurant, this is the case, so my lady and I went to sit down. Where we sat was fine but the only waiter who was willing to put his life on the front lines and work was quick to stop the elderly man from sitting were he wanted as the restaurant was doing that six foot people separation thing. He wanted him to sit at another booth a bit deeper in the restaurant. The old guy would not take no for answer. He began to loudly argue with the waiter about where he wanted to sit. Finally, I told him to take our table, as we were happy to sit father back in the restaurant.

It was there and then that I joking exclaimed to my lady about Rapture. Here we are, the damned, kept from heaven, having to deal with people like that.

Artistically, there has always been an allure about being one of the damned. You are cool, you are on the outside, you are a nonconformist. But, art and life rarely equal reality. Most people simply want to live a normal and well-awarded life. They do not want conflict, disaster, or to be forced to deal with unkind, unruly people.

Now, today, here we are, the ones living though this coronavirus situation. I would guess that some of the world communities are not as limited as to what they are allowed do by government proclamations as we are here in California—some are probably much worse. But, for those of us here and now and for those of you in the future who look back to this time, this is ideal example of how the actions of one small group of people, based in a food market in China, can come to dominate the entire globe and its population. The actions of one, two, or a few people can take control over other people's and the whole world's reality.

If you study the bible, whether you are a Christian or not, and you want an ideal physical example of the coming of Armageddon, (that is precisely detailed within its pages), you need look no further than what is taking place right now.

But, for the rest of us, he we are, stuck in this Rapture, being kept from doing what we want to do. Hoping that we do not contract the disease and become deathly ill. Many are being kept from earning their income and what is going to happen to them in the days, weeks, and months to come? Here we are, dealing with those who are not very nice, being guided towards fear by the government(s) and the media, and being controlled by a distant abstract power that we have no control over.

Thessalonians 4:16-18, *"For the Lord himself will come down from heaven, with a loud command, with the voice of the archangel and with the trumpet call of God, and the dead in Christ will rise first. After that, we who are still alive and are left will be caught up together with them in the clouds to meet the Lord in the air. And so we will be with the Lord forever. Therefore encourage one another with these words."*

Creating a State of Panic
16/Mar/2020 09:22 AM

As I look out over the horizon, it is a beautiful morning. There are still a few clouds in the sky from the recent rain and I am told some more rain is on its way. That's a good thing. Rain is a good thing. It is very cleansing. We always need rain.

Turn on the TV and the world is in crisis. The coronavirus COVID-19 is in control of the entire globe. There are all of the politicians vying for screen time. They get behind the podium, in front of the cameras, and spill out their discourses: some with big smiles on their face, others blaming others. It is really not a humanizing thing to do.

I did not think I would so quickly write another blog about this coronavirus but just last night the mayor of L.A. shut down all restaurants, bars, gyms, movie theaters, and the like throughout the city. Though I have not been going to the gym since the beginning of this whole episode, but restaurants, that really pops my bubble, as I eat in them all the time.

The politicians have been telling people to stop hoarding food, as there is plenty of it. The reasons the shelves in the supermarkets are bare is because they can't be restocked fast enough. But now, last night, the mayor in essence shuts down the entire city. What kind of reaction does he think that will invoke in the people? He and other politicians are creating a state of panic. All so they can look like they are in control and get screen time for their next reelection campaign.

Most people I encounter see all of this as much to do about nothing. Yet, there they are stockpiling groceries. And, being in disbelief when they can't find what they came to the store for on the shelves. All of this—the everything, this is just the wrong way to handle this situation.

As I spoke about in my first blog on the subject and the one yesterday what China has allowed to happen is controlling the world. China is in control of the world. I am sure there are some high-end politicians that are quite pleased with themselves. Having has some very interactive experiences with the powers-that-be in China, I know of what I speak. I have been to the sourcepoint of this coronavirus, the market in Wuhan, and like I said it my first blog on this subject, it is not a clean or healthy place.

I believe that a lot of people, who have never been to the open-air markets of Mainland China, do not understand what they are like. The locals eat rats, dogs, and all kinds of stuff that our western minds would find disgusting. Many of those animals sit in the market dead but uncooked. I am sure if you go online you can find videos of the Wuhan market and you can see what I am speaking about. Again, it is not a clean or healthy place.

I am not being a racist, a xenophobe, or anything like that. I am just stating the truth. Like I've said before, why is no one taking China to task about creating this global pandemic due to their unclean eating habits?

In any case, like in all life situations that are not ideal, we just have to do what we can do. We must remain conscious and be the sourcepoint for higher consciousness in all that we are dealt. The politicians are wrong in how they are handing this situation. China is wrong for letting their food market situations smolder for such a long period of time. The hoarders are wrong. They are keeping needed nutrition from the masses as they stock their shelves with food they will probably never eat and throw away once it expires.

The one good thing, remember that guy in Tennessee I mentioned yesterday, the one who stockpiled over seventeen thousands bottles of hand sanitizer, after law enforcement officials of Tennessee began an investigate into his price gouging, he donated all of the hand sanitizer. Keep your hands clean people of Tennessee.

In any moment that we find ourselves experiencing in life,

all we can be is all we can be. It is we who can make the choice to be positive, be strong, and do good things for others.

Take a moment right now—a moment as we are in the midst of this mess. Look out the window, see the sky, love the sky. Take a moment to be free. Let you mind study its beauty. If you have a pet, go love that pet. Pet them, do whatever it is they like. Make them feel special. If you are in a relationship—if you have kids or a family, tell them you love them. Let them know that you care. For this is what life is all about, being an interactive part of this world where we live, making someone else feel okay even when the world is not necessarily okay. For this is the definition of each of our lives, the truth of how we feel about others, the truth about what we do to and for others.

Be nice. Do good. Don't let your ego, your desires, or your panic drive your actions. Feel the perfect perfection of nature. And, love those you have been given the chance to love.

Pandemic 2020 Part 2
15/Mar/2020 08:09 AM

I don't know about where you live but where I live, in the greater Los Angeles area, ever since the outbreak of the coronavirus, COVID-19, the world has gone nuts. People have gone crazy. People are hoarding the all and the everything, there is fights in the supermarkets over toilet paper, and the shelves of many supermarkets have been left bare. Crazy… It doesn't have to be like this people!

I mean, I get it, people are panicked. But, I think it is more based in the fact that people want something to be panicked about. Many people have nothing, *"Big,"* in their life. They have nothing all-encompassing. So, when something like this comes around, it provides them with a purpose to react.

I had to go to the supermarket yesterday. First off all, though there were long lines, everybody was very-very nice. No pushing, no shoving, only, *"Excuse me."* Many of the shelves were bare. I posted some photos of it on my Yelp account. But, the thing is, many of the things that were gone have no reason to be gone. Like virtually all of the bottled water was gone. Normally, that is never the case. Meaning, most of the time the people who are buying all this bottled water are not normally drinking it.

There are a lot of people, including myself, who have spend much of their life attempting to drink the cleanest water possible. We drink bottled or filtered water. But, this is America people! The tap water is safe! You can drink water right out of the faucet and it is not going to hurt you! In fact, pretty much every time you are in a restaurant that is what you are drinking; unfiltered tap water.

The other thing I notice was that people have hoarded all of the bad food. The can goods were wiped out as was all the soup, Top Ramen, and stuff like that. But, the vegetable were untouched. Plenty of fresh, healthy vegetable. No one is buying them; except me.

I needed some butter and as I walked towards the butter case, it looked empty. When I got there, all the margarine and regular butter was gone. But, the unsalted butter, which is the kind I buy anyway, was fully stocked. Why in these times of pandemic does everyone focus on eating so unhealthy?

The toilet paper, in a way I get it... But, by hoarding it you are really messing with the lives of other people because there is none for them. And, doing anything against anybody is not right.

There was this one guy on Facebook who said he was going to the store to get some TP but when he got there he posted a photo of the fact that it was all gone. I don't know what he did because TP is kind of a necessity.

I think back to the time when I was living in India. Probably most people don't know this and never even thought about it but in India, particularly rural India, many people don't use toilet paper. I've had bicycle taxi drivers stop by the side of the road, lift their dhoti, squat down, take a shit, and then get up and get back on the bike and start pedaling. Me, I always carried a bandana or two with me and if there was no TP to be found I would use that and then wash it out. But here, people are hoarding the toilet paper and a lot of everything else and that is not good.

One of the most messed up things I've heard about in regard to hoarding is that this guy in Tennessee currently has over seventeen thousand bottles of hand sanitizer. When this whole thing started, he when around his city and state buying all the hand sanitizer he could find. He cleaned out the stores. Plus, he bought cases of hand sanitizer online. He then began selling them on Amazon and eBay and asking an exorbitant amount per bottle. He was trying to make major bank from these bottles by playing off of the fears of the people. How fucked up is that? But, Amazon and eBay shut him down for price gouging. As they should. Now, he is stuck with all that product—product that if it was in the hands of the people could perhaps keep them from getting COVID-19. One nurse they were interviewing in regard to this situation exclaimed, *"What an asshole."* And, he is. Another said, he should donate all of those bottles of hand sanitizers to nursing homes or hospitals. But, I doubt he will do that.

This guy was attempting to follow the old rule of business, buy low and sell high. But, by attempting to do that, especially in this situation, he has put a lot of people's lives at risk. What is the karma for that?

Mostly, this whole pandemic thing has brought out both the best and the worst in people. Like hand sanitizer; why weren't people using it in the first place?

I was in a restaurant a couple of days ago, speaking to the hostess who I know, discussing how she is on the front lines of all of this as she has so much customer interaction and she mentioned that now the restaurant is whipping down the tables and the menus with disinfectant all the time. My question, why weren't they doing that all along?

The airlines, now they are using HEPA filters. Why weren't they doing this all the time?

Sadly, some people have and will get sick from this coronavirus. Some people have and will die. There have been all kinds of movies made about this (possible) situation. But, now it is here. It is our reality. China can be very proud as what I am sure the politicians of that country have wanted for centuries, they are in control of the world—they have brought the world to its knees. But, as I mentioned in my previous blog about this pandemic, no one is bringing them to task. I don't know, somebody should be pissed.

The good news is, this pandemic will pass. Hopefully we will have learned and become better people because of it. Hopefully, but I doubt it. Today, people are still at the supermarkets hoarding. Are they caring about their neighbor or the person next to them in the store? Probably not. Just like the guy buying all the hand sanitizer that he could find to sell it for a major profit, he is only thinking about himself. Hopefully, he will get totally financially fucked for doing that. But, I doubt that too. Somebody will probably buy his hoard from him, so they can sell it to their customers. At least then it will be out helping the masses instead of sitting in a garage until it meets its expiration date.

    People; care! Be better! Do good things for other people! Be nice! And, if you can, always lend a helping hand. Let all this be a wake up call for you to become a better person who thinks about the other person instead of only thinking about yourself.

Faith
13/Mar/2020 09:14 AM

I was sitting in a restaurant the other day, having lunch with my lady. There was this conversation going on next to me. One of those conversations that you wish you didn't have to listen to but they are talking so loudly that you do not have a choice. The one guy, talking the loudest and the most, was this actor who had hit his stride in the 1970s and I haven't seen much of him since then. He was telling the man, sitting across the table from him, this very embellished story about how his faith had guided him to travel to India but while there he had a long talk with god telling god that he wasn't seeking a new religion as he had all he needed in Christianity so he pulled out his bible, read it, and decided to come home.

Have you ever been around one of those people in a restaurant (or elsewhere) and you can tell that they are talking not in the manner that they only want the person or persons they are with to hear them but they want the all and the everyone to hear what they have to say as they feel what they are saying is so fucking important? This was one of those cases. The guy loudly went on and on about his love for god and faith. It really killed by dining experience. But, as most events like this do, it got me to thinking…

Faith is an interesting beast. What is faith? Basically it is a person believing in something where they are provided with absolutely no concrete proof of the existence of what they are believing in. Ministers will tell you when you have doubts to, "Just believe, have faith, and any doubt will pass." But, that is a strange concept, don't you think? Believing in something that by its very nature is intangible. Yet, all across the globe that is exactly what people do.

Sure, there are tons of passages in the bible that define faith, 2 Corinthians 5:7, *"For we walk by faith not by sight,"*

Mark 11:22-24, *"So Jesus answered and said to them, 'Have faith in God. For assuredly, I say to you, whoever says to this mountain, 'Be removed and be cast into the sea,' and does not doubt in his heart, but believes that those things he says will be done, he will have whatever he says. Therefore I say to you, whatever things you ask when you pray, believe that you receive them, and you will have them."* And, the list goes on and on.

In Islam, the idea of faith is often referred to by the Arabic word, *"Al-iman."* In the Koran, Surat An-Nisa 4:136 states, *"O you who believe, have faith in Allah and His messenger and the book that He revealed to His messenger and the scripture which He revealed before. Whoever disbelieves in Allah, His angels, His books, His messengers, and the Last Day has certainly gone far astray."*

Though Buddhism should be devoid of faith, at least in terms of the sense of idol worship, nonetheless, countless Buddhists pray to the image of the Buddha all the time.

Faith is everywhere. People believe. People need to believe. People are feed things to believe in. They are fed the promises of what their belief will equal: a good life, success, happiness, wealth, relationships, peace, heaven, and the list goes on. When people believe and their desires are not met, they are told they are being tested. But tested by whom, I always questioned. Tested why? Does god have the time to test all of us just in the way that will mess up our lives the most?

People are also provided with examples of what faith will deliver, *"Look at that person, they believed and look how good their life turned out."*

But mostly, what I always see, is that the person who is telling the people to have faith is the person who is gaining something from the telling, whether that something is the money they get from the collection plate, the sense of power it gives them to guide and be in control over other people, or the ability to appear to be something and know something more that others do not. In other words, faith is a game of power, ego, and money.

I'm not being cynical here, nor am I being judgmental. I get it... People need something to believe in. The question is, *"Why?"* Why do people need something to believe in? It is something innate to our nature or is it something that was programmed into us?

I know for me, from my earliest memories forward I was taught to believe, to pray, and to have faith. I am certain that was the case with my parents and my parent's parents, as well. So, is faith instinctive or is it programmed into us and why? Do you ever ask yourself that question?

Think about your life... Think if you were never taught that there was supposedly a god, by whatever faith you were brought up in. If you were not taught to believe, what would you believe in? If you were not told you should have faith, would you possess any faith?

The thing is, most people never ponder the subtleties of their life and/or their life beliefs. They are just taught to believe, so they believe. They are just taught what religion to follow, so that is what they do. They do, but they do not think about what they do or why they do it.

Take a little time... Think about what you believe and why you believe it. Think about what faith you possess and why you have faith in that whatever in the first place. Think about it and perhaps you will emerge with a new life definition.

*   *   *

12/Mar/2020 12:24 PM

What do they do in heaven?

The Sane Can Go Crazy but the Crazy Can Never Go Sane
12/Mar/2020 07:58 AM

There is this large intersection not far from where I live. There are shopping plazas on all four sides of it. As I often pass through this intersection and am often held at the stop light for a minute or two it forever provides an interesting glimpse into local life.

Maybe ten years ago I began to notice this woman walking in the vicinity of this intersection. The reason I took notice of her is that she was always dressed like and had the same hairstyle as Madonna in the 1980s. She would walk around with a dance in her step. I could tell she was a bit off and suffering from OCD as she would always walk around in circles several times when she passed this one man hole cover. Time went on and I didn't see Madonna anymore. Her image had completely faded from my mind.

A week or two ago I was in one of the stores in one of the shopping plaza bounded by that aforementioned intersection. I was looking around and I noticed a woman looking at me. She was not unattractive. Maybe late forties with long blonde hair. The main thing I noticed about her was that she was dressed like Stevie Nicks in the 1970s. I didn't give the situation much thought. I continued my shopping.

A few minutes later the lady walks up next to me. She was talking to herself. She was having this whole ongoing discussion about whether or not she should buy a man's suit, as maybe it would make her look, *"Pretty good."* Immediately, I realized who she was. She was the once Madonna girl who had now, apparently, transitioned to Stevie Nicks. From a distance, she looked totally normal but up close, she was bleeding mad. She was insane but she was functioning; barely. Where she had been these past years, I have no idea but now she is back as a new character devised only in her own mind.

This is the thing, the insane never become sane. At best they are maintained by medication. Certainly, their condition is not their fault. It is biology, it is trauma, it is whatever... But, once one has been etched with a mental pattern, it never changes.

All the time, all over the place, people are traumatized by tragic life events and it causes them to be driven down a dark psychological pathway. They will be forever defined by that event.

Has someone ever done something to you that defined your psychological makeup for the rest of your life? How did you feel about that? How do you feel about that? Have you ever unleashed something that hurt someone to the degree that it came to be a defining factor in his or her psychological makeup? How did you feel about that? How do you feel about that?

Have you ever been diagnosed with a condition: medical or psychological, that you wished you did not have? How have you lived with that condition since your diagnosis?

Life is a case study in acceptable psychology. Life is a case study in adaptation. Life is a case study in charting reality. Some people's reality is different from other people's reality. Most are pretty much the same, and then there are those few who marginally function but walk among us.

Where are you on that scale of psychology, adaptation, and reality? What does it cause you to do? How does it cause you to react?

We are all going to pass through our lives one way or the other. Some people are blessed and provided with the opportunity to do good things. Others have many an obstacle to overcome. But, at the end of the day, all we are is all we are. We are created, we are born, we live, and then we die. What we live is all that we are. What we do in the time frame of life is all that we do. For some, we attempt to be in control and define our own reality even if we must fight psychological demons. For others, all they are left with is a distorted imitation of what they hoped their reality could be.

Who are you? What have you lived? What have you created? What have you done to yourself? What have you done to others? What has what you've done, done to reality?

Are you living a truth or are you only living a projected imitation of who you wished you could be?

The sane can go crazy but the crazy can never go sane.

* * *

12/Mar/2020 07:57 AM

Most people who are unhappy never want to admit to themselves that is was their own choices and actions that is the cause of their unhappiness.

How You Live. Why You Live. What You Live.
11/Mar/2020 09:12 AM

Like the old saying goes, *"Out of the mouths of babes…"* What I always find is that we can learn a lot from people just saying the nothing that is so common in everyday conversation. It provides us with essential food for thought.

I was watching a reality TV show a year or two ago and this one cast member said, in regard to another cast member, *"He lives like a junior college student."* That statement really struck me because how does a junior college student live? I imagine we all have our own impression of what that means, but to me it means living a not very established existence in a place that is perhaps a little messy and not all that great.

I think back to when I was in junior college—although here, in California, they call them community colleges. I went to Los Angeles Pierce College before graduating and going on to CSUN. Back then, in the 1970s, it was considered one of the most fun places to go to college for those of us, like myself, who were not academically inclined. Though I went to school during the day, my mind was really elsewhere. It was focused on spirituality and music. I just did the bare minimum to get through my classes. During this time period, I rented a small apartment not far from campus. It was kinda funky but it was a place to live. There it housed my guitars, my amps, and my 4 Track reel-to-reel recording system.

How a person lives is really an interesting presentation into their mind. It truly allows us to understand their life definitions and their life motivations. As we pass through life, if we have an eye for it, we can truly learn a lot by studying the WHY of other people. From this, it provides us with not only a deeper understanding of human reality but it also provides us with a way to come to better understand ourselves while presenting us with a method to chart our own destiny.

Once upon a time, everybody who lived in one area pretty much all lived the same. Defined by environment and the means of sustenance that environment provided, all who existed there possessed a fairly common lifestyle. Now, a person living next door to an individual may be living an entirely different existence. Though in the same vicinity, how they live and what they do to live may be completely different.

As I have passed through my years I have known many people living many ways. In fact, having spent most of my adult years being closely associated with the Korean and the Korean American community I have seen how culture plays a large part in a person's living situation. For example, though most in the Korean American community are happy to live at home with their parents until they get married, once they do a house is either purchased for them or they are given a large down payment for a home of their choosing. That's a great thing. How you are set up in life really sets the stage for your later existence. It really helps. I wish someone had done that for me. Nobody ever gave me anything.

In my life, I have known hoarders who live in perpetuated clutter. I had one friend who wouldn't even let me into his house any more when I went to pick him up because it was so over run with junk. Important stuff to someone but to no one else. I have known trust fund babies who get to live a great existence, in grand homes, but they have done nothing to earn it. I have known people who got a big inheritance and lived the carefree life until they blew through it. I have known people who have spent their whole existence living in one small apartment where they raised their children. Working but never making enough money to move up. I have known women who have married men, divorced them, and got to keep the great house the man worked so hard to provide. Then, by never marrying again, they got alimony checks for the rest of their days. I know a man who is doing that right now based on the money of his ex-wife. Not cool! I have one friend who is in his forties and another one who is in his late fifties living with their mothers. No money, no job, doing nothing to better themselves all day. One of the guys has been doing this for like ten years. I just do not know how someone can live like that. I've also known people who have gone bankrupt because of where they lived.

Where you live, how you live, and why you live there really provides a microscope into the life of a person. Many make excuses for where they live, how they live, and why they live the way that they do. Some are just in flat out denial about why they live the way that they do. Ask a person why they live the way they do and what they say will provide you with a deep understanding of who and what that person truly is. All you have to do is listen to their reasons. Is it the truth? Is it a lie? Is it an excuse? Is it the truth based only in the mind of that one person?

Most of us have to work to survive. Most of us have to work to have a place to live. And, it is not easy to find a way to find a means of sustenance. For those of us who care about things like karma, not hurting people and/or the environment by doing what we do, and perhaps making the world a little bit better place while earning a living, the choices are even more few and far between.

All this equals one thing. How a person lives, how a person chooses to live, what a person does to give themselves a place to live, and how that doing affects them and the everything else comes to be the defining factor of a person's life.

How do you live? Where do you live? What do you do inside of where you live? Why do you live there? Just as in all things in life if you do not possess a valid definition for what you do and why you do what you do you are living a life devoid of consciousness and interpersonal understanding. If you want to understand others, study others. If you want to understand yourself, know why you live where you live.

* * *

11/Mar/2020 09:12 AM

How much does what you think really matter?

*   *   *
11/Mar/2020 09:11 AM

How much of what you've done do you wish you could erase?

* * *

11/Mar/2020 09:10 AM

You can't make a person care about you if they don't care about you.

Did You Know I Love to Dance
10/Mar/2020 09:09 AM

Like I have long said, (and even written a blog about back in the first incarnation of the Scott Shaw Zen Blog), *"Nobody likes to see an old person dance."* This realization was brought to my attention when back in maybe 1990 I was at a nightclub with my girlfriend and this well-known newscaster, from a local TV station, came in with his wife and they begun to trip the light fantastic. Good newscaster but you just didn't want to see him dance.

Even before that, my longtime party bud Vinchenzo and I would go to this dance oriented metal club on Tuesday nights, *The Cathouse*. …For years we used to go out virtually every night of the week. Back then, the L.A. clubs were each a one-night a week thing. One night they would be one club, the next another. Anyway… So, we had our spots per night picked out. Each week at *The Cathouse* there was this one old dude: very old, very grey, but he would get out there and dance all night by himself. He looked to be an old hippie and maybe that had something to do with it. …Too many drugs and all… But, he would go there solo and dance and dance and dance. Good exercise, I guess. And, fun for him. But, it was not easy to witness.

Since way back in the days of Punk and New Wave, Vinchenzo and I always hit the dance floors of the clubs. Even though we are white, I believe we both possessed a strong since of rhythm.

Dancing was and is great. It was a great way to meet girls. And, it is fun. I love it. I remember this one time I was in a club in Beijing and I danced so long with this girl that I literally stopped sweating. I knew that could not be good but I continued to dance.

I was even hired as a dancer in this one Kid 'n Play movie, *House Party 2,* way back in the way back when. They hired another actor and myself because, I believe, we had long hair and could dance. Long hair was all the rage back then. …It was a whole audition thing I had to go through and all that. If I remember correctly, I don't think you can see that other guy and myself in the final cut of film, however, though they did spend a lot of time shooting our dance moves. …They cut us out probably because we were white. No big deal. That's Hollywood. It was fun. I met a nice girl, (but that's a whole other story). And, I got paid handsomely. Plus, I got to dance all day…

Anyway, I love to dance…

But, then came age. Then, came the reality of knowing who and what I am. Old. (No matter how young I may feel). Does that change my love for dance? No. Now, when a great beat comes on the TV in some show I am watching I'm always moving my arm rhythmically in the air and swaying to the music. But, I just don't make any one witness it. No one except maybe my lady. Poor girl.

Life goes on. We all love what we love when we are young. It's not that the love for that something ever changes; it is just that we change and we have to be very aware of that change. We have to be what we are when we are.

This is the thing that many people never realize and what causes so many people to have so many regrets and live an unfulfilled existence. They do not evolve with time. They do not let themselves be what they are when they are. They hold onto something back there/back then and instead of living their moment as best as it can be lived they lock themselves into a mindset of who they used to be and what they miss about who they used to be.

This occurs in both a positive and a negative manner. Some people are in love with the life they used to live. It defines them. Some people are locked into a bad experience that happened to them back then. It defines them. But, in either case, though it is impossible to forget who we used to be, what we used to do, and what situations occurred to us because of that fact, here we are in this moment. Here we are in this now. This is our reality. Not the once was.

If you lock yourself into that past, you can never truly experience this present. It is as simply as that. Sure, I loved to dance. Sure, I look back to those days with happy thoughts. But, I do not let them control my now. And, neither should you.

Be what you are when you are. Be the best you can be in your moment. Know who you are in your moment. But, never let your vision of what you used to be cloud the perfection of your now.

* * *

10/Mar/2020 07:36 AM

Even the small things are an adventure if you see the experience for what it truly is.

* * *
09/Mar/2020 07:27 AM

Before you ever ask anyone for anything ask yourself what are you going to do for them.

The Experiencing of Everything
08/Mar/2020 08:10 AM

For each of us there are those moments when we encounter something new; see it or feel it for the first time. Those moments are very special. They cause us to step back from all of the nonsense that is going on in our brains—all our thinking and simply witness the perfection of the newness.

For each of us there are those moments when we encounter something that we have seen before but for some reason it all seems so new. It is like we have never seen it before. Those moments are very special. They cause us to step back from all of the nonsense that is going on in our brains—all our thinking and simply witness the perfection of the newness.

The way you live your life; the things you encounter in your life are both presented in a pattern of expectation and realization. You live your life. You do the things you do. You do the things you always do and from that you will see the things you always see, encounter the people you always encounter, and feel the same feelings motivated by what you encounter.

Then, there is the something new. This may occur by accident or by choice. You may just be doing what you always do and all of sudden the new, the different finds you. If you have the mind for it, these moments are very special. They are the times that lead to new enhanced experience and new knowledge.

There are also the new experiences that you choose to encounter. You hear of something, you are told about something, and you move outwards from your expected reality and encounter that which is new. In any of these cases, the new changes you forever because now you have become something more by encountering something different. This is what leads to life evolution.

All this being said, there is one final roadway to encountering the new. That pathway is a mental corridor where you choose to see and experience something for the first time—something you have seen and/or done before.

Think about it—think about your life, how many things do you do on a daily basis but never think about? You have done them, you have seen them so many times that encountering them does not cause your mind to do anything.

Here's the meditation… Stop right now and look around. Look at where you find yourself. Study where you find yourself. Open up. Listen, smell, look, and feel. Do this as if it is the first time you have ever encountered the where you are. What are you experiencing? What is what you are experiencing causing you to feel?

Now, look at something. Maybe you have seen that object a million times but look at it as if you were seeing it for the first time. Study it. Look at it as if you have never seen it before. Experience it as if you are seeing it for the first time.

Yes, we all live what we live on a daily basis. Many of the things we encounter we have seen or felt a million times. But, there is newness in all things. There is realization that can be gained from all things known or unknown. There is new knowledge that can be recognized from all things no matter how many times we have seen them before.

Take the time to wake up to the new. Take the time to re-see things for the first. Take the time to newly experience all the things you thought you knew. Do this and a whole new world of inspired realization opens up for you.

Dead Dudes Don't Die
07/Mar/2020 07:33 AM

    The Jim Jarmusch movie, *The Dead Don't Die* was on Cinemax last night so I thought I would sit back and watch it. Though Jarmusch has forever been known for his creative filmmaking, I was very surprised to see some of the things he did in this film like shooting Day for Night, referencing the fact that they were actually shooting a movie in the dialogue several times, and resorting to humor like the fact of Bill Murray stating that he had done a lot for, *"Jim,"* and Adam Driver having a *Star Wars* keychain and referencing the film, etc… I always find that kind of in-movie humor a bit contrived like when De Niro looks in a mirror and says, *"You look'n at me,"* in his later films, Willis saying, *"Yippee ki yay,"* or Arnold saying, *"I'll be back."* But, that's just me…

    The main thing that caught me about this film was its title. …Obviously a play on all the zombie TV and movie filmmaking that is going on in this day and age.

    The interesting thing, at least to me, is back in '92 I put out a casting notice for my next film as, *Dead Dudes Don't Die*. I still have a clipping of that casting notice somewhere. I should find it, pull it out, and scan it or something. This title was obviously a tongue in cheek idea and I wasn't really going to use that title for the film that became *Samurai Ballet*. But, it was at a time when a filmmaker had to be kind of careful in the indie film industry as people would often confiscate your ideas.

    Back then, it was a very different world in cinema and cinema creation here in Hollywood. Everybody, including me, paid a lot of money to have headshots taken, then you paid to have them duplicated. You got your resume together, had it printed at Kinkos or some similar place, stapled it onto the back of your 8 X 10 headshot, and then every Thursday, when the casting newspaper *Dramalogue* came out, you would go to the newsstand and buy a copy, look through it, find the roles that you believed suited you, put your headshot and resume in a manila envelope, put a stamp (or two) on it, and mail it out. All that cost a lot of money. I don't even know how much money I spent in that era. But, it was a lot. I had the same hopes as everybody else. The hope of, *"Making it."* The only difference was, between the time I got into the industry as an actor and when I became a filmmaker was a relatively short period of time.

In any case, when I choose that title, I was really curious to see how people would respond. …Because it was such an off the wall title. In fact, I was surprised at how many personalized responses I got. Again, back then, it was a different world. People cared. Peopled tried. People just didn't expect it to be handed to them. People were willing to do the work.

I got tons of personal handwritten notes, in regard to that casting notice, telling me how the actor or actress really wanted to be in the film, *Dead Dudes Don't Die.* I guess I should have kept all of those notes. But, I rarely keep anything.

Anyway, to the point of all this… I think it is so interesting/funny how as we walk through time how the world evolves and how what we thought, did, or envisioned as a joke can become part of the mainstream. Moreover, I see how through time many people have become complacent in regard to what they hope to achieve—especially in the film industry. Few seem willing to try. And, this goes to all things in life, not just acting. If you want to achieve you have to try. It is not going to be handed to you. If you want to, *"Make it,"* you've got to take the time to write that personalized note and send it out with your headshot and resume even if the movie has a ridiculous title. Because if you don't try and you don't try really hard how can you ever expect to achieve anything? …And then, you never know, maybe an idea you had as a joke can find its way to the mainstream.

Pandemic 2020
04/Mar/2020 07:10 AM

Ever since the coronavirus, COVID-19, has been sweeping the globe people are becoming increasing paranoid about all that they are doing. And, rightly so. Here in L.A. I heard on the news yesterday how virtually every store is sold out of antibacterial gel. Luckily, I have a few stashed in the drawer as I have forever carried and used that stuff. How far this coronavirus will spread and how many it will kill is anybody's guess but this type of unseen, unwanted attack can come at us at any time.

From the time I was a young undergraduate student, studying my major, Cultural Geography, at CSUN, I was taught that whenever any population becomes over crowded, sooner or later, seventy-five percent of that population will die off due to either starvation or disease. And, this is an example of that happening. The problem is, once upon a time, that type of population attack happened only within a specific cultural. Now, due to the world having become so small and people traveling everywhere, anything they contract, they spread. And, as we are witnessing, it spreads very quickly.

It is said that this coronavirus was born in a market in Wuhan China. From what I've read, researchers believe that this virus, the Zoonotic Virus, occurred because of the eating of pangolin. Now, I am not being ethnocentric, racist, or judgmental here, but if you have ever been to the markets in China most of them are filthy. I mean, I get it… It's a cultural thing and people get their food there everyday and they have done so for eons. But, those markets are not clean or sterile. If you haven't seen one face-to-face look them up online. Sure, they are visually interesting. I film and take photographs in them virtually any time I am in one. But, there is no doubt about how this is the birthplace of pandemic diseases like COVID-19, SARS, MERS, or H1N1.

The thing that I believe is interesting is that everybody in the world gets mad at other countries for doing what they do. If a volcano erupts and messes up air travel everybody is pissed at that country and they want to fine them. But, that is a natural occurrence. It is no ones fault. People get pissed off at the political entities in countries that go and attack other countries or in the case of civil war their own people. They place sanctions on that country or maybe even attack. But, why is no one pissed off at China? Why is no one telling them they must change their food practices? Because what they have done and what they are doing has and is killing people.

 Nobody wants to catch a disease. Nobody wants to die. Nobody wants the people they love or care about to die. But, when an attack like this comes at us, so unseen, there is only so much we can do, as we never know where the attack will come from.

 I don't mean to get philosophical here but more than just a truth of over population this COVID-19 thing illustrates how life is forever unseen. Kind of like the mugger hiding in the shadows or the troll on the internet we can get attacked and never see it coming, so how much self-defense can we practice for?

 You know, we are all going to live and we are all going to die. Living is great but dying is always sad. It is the end that no one wants. And, if this dying comes simply because someone can't keep their supermarkets clean that is very-very sad.

 All we can do is all we can do. Be good. Be clean. Be protected. But know, sometimes life attacks you and you never see it coming. Be prepared for the un-preparable.

* * *

04/Mar/2020 07:10 AM

When someone has a dream and you are in it, is that really you?

*　　*　　*
04/Mar/2020 07:09 AM

People always talk about what they gave you but no one wants to speak about what they took away.

*   *   *

03/Mar/2020 08:50 AM

What if you didn't care?

The Illusion of Money
03/Mar/2020 07:27 AM

  This 2020 presidential race, here in the United Stated, has provided an interesting look into finances and the mind of those with money. For example, this one candidate, who just dropped out of the race, spent an estimated two hundred million dollars of his own money to run for president. Before that he spent millions running commercials, with himself front and center, to impeach the president. This, before the democrats even launched their attempted at doing the same thing. Does no one understand the process of impeachment in the U.S.? Nonetheless, this man, who has a lot of money, spent a lot of money. But, for what? What did it accomplish? What did it prove?

  Think about that amount of money; two hundred million, don't you think you could have lived a really good life if you had that much money? I know I could have lived a really good existence, from birth to death, with that amount. Yet, this guy just blew it.

  There's another candidate who has spent an estimated five hundred million dollars of his own money, so far, running for president. Yes, so far. And, he's not even done spending. There are constantly commercials of his face on TV. But, to what end? Spending to spend? Ego? I know more, I have more, thus I am more than you?

  Money is a curious thing in life. We all need it to survive. We all must find a way to get it. But, within that it becomes such a controlling element of our minds, our actions, and our life. Think about the things people have done to get money. Think about how they have hurt themselves and how they have hurt others. How about you? What have you done to get money? Who have you hurt in the process?

  And, that is the thing about the acquisition of money, in many cases, people are hurt in the process of obtaining it. Then, people are hurt when they have it no more.

Money it an undefined variable. It is an energy constant. It is continually moving and flowing. But, the capture of it is only mastered by the very few. Then, what do they do with it? Many do nothing more than spend it on feeding their ego.

Think about the money you have had. What have you spent it on? Did you buy yourself nice clothes? …A nice car? … A nice place to live? Did you take people out with your money trying to impress them? Or, did you simply spend it on yourself trying to make you look like a bigger you or a more famous you?

There is the day-to-day need of money for survival. But, beyond that the whole ideology of money gets very convoluted.

The percentage of Americans living paycheck-to-paycheck is estimated to be seventy-eight percent. That is over three quarters of this country that if they lose their job they have no money in the bank. Then, what happens to them? How about you?

Then there is debt. How many people are in debt paying insane credit card interest just because they wanted something that they could not afford? Again, what does the need for money and the desire to be more and have more lead people to do in terms of money? Some try to buy the presidency.

I think most of us have known people who have had a lot of money. Probably most of us have known people who should have had money but they do not. Having been in the film game for so many years by this point in my life I have known so many known actors who one would think that they should be living really well but they are not. They are broke, they are couch surfing, they are living with their parents, or they are working menial jobs.

I knew this one famous faced actor who went to work at a restaurant near where I live. He worked there as a waiter with many of the customers recognizing him. He worked there until one day I heard the manager confronting him about stealing money from the safe. Then, he worked there no more.

Money makes people do crazy things. Everybody wants it and it is foremost in many people's mind. But, once they have it or once they need it everything goes crazy and they do senseless things.

I remember this one time that an author spoke about my Zen Films and me in one of his books. I told this one actor friend about this fact, as I thought he would be happy to know that his name was mentioned. His first word, *"How much am I going to get paid?"* Nothing. You don't paid just because somebody writes about you. But, that's were everybody's mind goes. *"How much am I going to get paid?"*

So, what does all this tell us about life and the life of money? It tells us that it is a control factor. It tells us that it is a desired factor. It tells us that it causes people to have their life dominated by its pursuit. It tells us that though some people do good things with the money they have, most do nothing more than stroke their own ego.

Here's the question(s)... What has money caused you to do? What has the desire for money caused you to do? What has the pursuit of life ego caused you to do in association with money?

Have you helped people because of money and/or its pursuit? Have you hurt people because of money and/or its pursuit?

Life is a complied thing. That is why it is a challenge. It challenges you to be the best you can be and do the best that you can do. The problem is, most people don't take on that challenge. They just do what they do to get what they want and everybody else be dammed. Thus, everywhere you look you will see people doing things that hurt other people so that they can get money. You will see people not caring about what they do to others because of their pursuit or spending of money. Ultimately, the only answer is in you—you who can choose to see money in a different light and instead of pursing it or pursing what it will bring you at any cost, use any of it that you have or you get as a tool to make everyone's everything better in any small way that you can.

Life is a challenge. It is what you do with the challenge that will define your existence at the end of your days. Do you want to live a meaningless life, defined by the money you have or the money you pursue, while feeding your own ego and/or wasting your Life Time or do you want to use money as an energy tool to make everyone's everything just a little bit better.

Control it or it controls you. It is really a very simple equation.

* * *
27/Feb/2020 07:22 AM

If you were to get rid of everything that you don't use how much stuff would you have left?

* * *

26/Feb/2020 03:16 PM

The done can't be undone but the undone never has to happen.

The Beliefs That You Believe
25/Feb/2020 07:57 AM

Pretty much everybody believes in something. Even those who claim that they don't believing in anything believe in that something; nothing.

Belief is the cornerstone of human reality. It makes us who and what we are.

We believe in that something and that something guides us to action. In guides us in what we say to others. In guides us in what we do to others. It guides us in what we do to ourselves.

Most people simply believe in what they believe in. Maybe what they believe in a big religious thing, maybe it is a movement, maybe it is the person that they love, or maybe it something very small. But, what they believe defines the reality of their life.

People who believe in that bigger something can easily find mutual believers. They can go to church, they can go to a concert, they can go to gathering. For them, life is much easier as finding a mutual believer is not difficult. The people who believe in the smaller things, for them there is often conflict, for they believe but they have no proof only their belief.

I was in a restaurant in Orange County the other night. It is one of those restaurants that has been around for decades but it changed its location maybe twenty-five years ago. I used to go to that one every now and then and now I go to this one every now and then.

All of a sudden I hear the hostess getting into it with this one guy. She is saying, *"Yes, he did come here! He came here all the time back in the 1960s. Jim Morrison was in here all the time!"* All this made me smile.

Think about it, sadly, how many people, in this day and age, even know who Jim Morrison (the singer for *The Doors*) actually was? He died in 1971. Unless you are of a certain age, he has all but been forgotten. If a person listens to oldies radio they might know the songs, *Light My Fire,* or *Hello, I Love You,* but other than that most never understand what a cultural revolutionary he was. Hell, Oliver Stone even made a movie about him.

When I was growing up my friends and I were really into *The Doors.* Sure, they sometimes did pop music but, via Morrison, they also proclaimed a lot of transcendence.

But, there she was, this young girl, maybe late teens or early twenties, arguing tooth and nail, claiming that he used to go into that restaurant. He probably died before her parents were born. Me, I doubt it. He hung out in Hollywood and Venice, but OC, that was a different world back then. It still is. But, she believed; she really believed. Why? Who knows? Where did she get the information to form her belief? Don't know that either. But, that or nothing else could change what she believed. And, she was willing to go to war over her belief.

But, here's the question, where is the proof? And, this is question that YOU always need to ask yourself whenever anyone tells you anything. Where is the proof? Because if there is no proof, there is no truth. If there is no truth and you are believing it —if there is no proof and you are fighting for your belief, what does that make you? Answer, it makes you nothing more than a fool.

Zen Filmmaking and All the Crazy Things That People Say
24/Feb/2020 08:32 AM

Note: Recently, I had an idea to put together a collection of the film reviews written about my Zen Film over the years. I titled it, *"Zen Filmmaking and All the Crazy Things That People Say."*

I put the book together. But then, I began to question whether or not I should have the book published. I don't know? Maybe I will, maybe I won't? But, for right now, here is the First Draft introduction to the book. Enjoy!

Introduction

Here's a fun book for all you fans (or haters) of *Zen Filmmaking*. Collected within these pages are many of the reviews of Zen Films that were posted on the internet over the years. Some are very positive, understanding, and praise the Zen Films while other (most) torpedo them proclaiming how horrible every aspect of every film actually is. In either case, combined, they present a fun, explicit look into the Zen craziness that is *Zen Filmmaking*. Read on and have fun.

*   *   *

Over the years since I entered the film game it has forever perplexed me how film reviewers, (professional and amateur), would take all the time and expend all of the energy necessary to write a review about an independent film they loved or hated. Of course, the reviews written by a hater of a film are always the most palpable but sometime people really love a film and write a strikingly positive review, as well. Personally, I always wondered why a reviewer would write a review instead of being imaginative in their own right and creating their own works of film art. But, that's just me…

I have always found it very disingenuous for a person who had not actually gone through the process of creating a film to become a film reviewer. Like I have long said, *"What is a film critic? With very few exceptions it is a person who doesn't have the talent or the dedication to actually create a film."* …For if a person has not actually created a film they have no idea about the process involved and what it takes to actually envision, instigate, get the equipment, the cast and the crew together, film and then edit, soundtrack, M&E the feature, and then realize a final production. If they have never had this experience, how can they truly understand filmmaking and how can they provide a valid commentary about a film without personally understanding what it took to bring that film together? Moreover, if they were not on the specific set of the film they are discussing they have no firsthand knowledge about what actually took place or what was the motivations of the filmmaker or the experiences of the cast or the crew.

Since my early emersion in the film industry I have felt the same way as many a filmmaker has, *"It's easy to discuss what someone else has done. Let's see what you can do."* Alas, most film critics never walk down the path of creative filmmaking, however, as it is so much easier to simply sit and type on their computer's keyboard or get in front of their iMac and discuss the productions of someone else.

Over the years I have watched as many a reviewer spoke about my Zen Films and myself. Many have actually attempted to tell their readers or listeners what I was feeling when I was creating a specific film. But, how can anyone know what another individual is feeling or why they do what they do? In virtually every case that a reviewer has spoken about my filmmaking motivations and the reasoning behind my end results, they were wrong. Wrong, but as a film critic in this day and age of self-publishing and internet forums, they encountered no checks and balances, so they could say whatever they want with no repercussions.

Some critics have even discussed how I felt about a specific review. I always found those statements immensely amusing. They never spoke to me—they never asked me how I felt... In fact, to this day, over all these many-many years and all of the films I have created, there has not been one film critic who actually spoke to me before or after they reviewed one of my movies. So, how could any of them have any idea about what I was feeling or why? The fact is, though a number of reviewers have discussed how I felt about a specific review, they were, in fact, wrong.

Do negative reviews bother me? I do not like negativity on any level for all it breeds is further negativity, nor do I appreciate reviewers who distort or twist the truth to their own ends in their reviews. This being said, if a review is well written, be it positive or negative, for the most part, I find them entertaining.

The thing I do not like, and I have spoken about this a lot over the years, is when a reviewer presents their opinion as fact but their opinion is, in fact, incorrect. What happens from this is that it provides a certain type of individual, who does not possess an investigative mind and does not scrutinize the supposed facts for themselves, to be exposed to falsehoods by believing the fabrications presented by the critic. This style of pseudo journalism gives birth to all kinds of misinformation and false facts being disseminated to the masses. Lies and falsehoods, based upon erroneous opinions, are a never a good thing.

I have long been an outspoken proponent of Intellectual Property Rights enforced by Copyright Law. In this digital age, most people don't care about the rights of the creator, however, as they just want to watch movies for free on unauthorized websites and grab footage from films and do whatever they want with it. Like I always say, if they were the creator of that film, they would possess a very different frame of mind, but as they are not, they do not care about the consequences this style of behavior has on the filmmaker. In fact, some on-line reviewers have become very wealthy grabbing footage from films without authorization and using that footage to create presentations. Illegal, yes. But, prosecution is very expensive, so many get away with it.

As the FBI has proclaimed, *"Internet Piracy is not a Victimless Crime."* The independent filmmaker is the one who is hurt. But, how many reviewers care as long as they are developing a following and making money off of discussing the creations of other people. And, how many viewers actually care as long as they are getting away with watching movies for free and/or being entertained by being allowed to watch or read provocative presentations based upon someone's opinion about someone else's creation?

Ever since I first created *Zen Filmmaking* it has always been about the lack of defined content. It is about freedom. It is about taking the viewer on a Mind Ride. It was never about story, story structure, or filming or acting in the traditional sense of the subject.

Since its inception, I have been very specific about what *Zen Filmmaking* was and what it was not. Yet, no matter how much information is out there about this cinematic art form, reviewers continue to get it wrong. They continue to attempt to define Zen Films within their own mental framework. They continue to attempt to put their own definition upon it and draw their own conclusion about it, comparing it to what it is not; traditional filmmaking.

Here lies the ultimate fault in the reviewer; they are attempting to put their own definition onto something that they can never truly understand. As they did not create it, they can never understand it. Thus, all they have to say about any film is solely based upon their own predetermined judgment about that film.

But remember, as it is proclaimed in Matthew 7:1-5,

"Judge not, that you be not judged. For with the judgment you pronounce you will be judged, and with the measure you use it will be measured to you. Why do you see the speck that is in your brother's eye, but do not notice the log that is in your own eye? Or how can you say to your brother, 'Let me take the speck out of your eye,' when there is the log in your own eye? You hypocrite, first take the log out of your own eye, and then you will see clearly to take the speck out of your brother's eye."

With all this as a basis, what I am presenting in this book are reviews about my films and my filmmaking taken from the Public Domain of the World Wide Web. As everybody seems to not care about the Copyright Infraction they have done to my films and my other creative works presented in their reviews, I will hereby return the favor.

What I am doing in this book is presenting you, the reader, with the reviews and the discourses, created by film critics that have been found and referred to me by friends, foes, and fans. They are presented in their entirety with no editing in any manner.

If any of you reviewers out there have a problem with this book, think about his, I am casting your reviews to the annals of history this one and only time. There will not be a second edition. Plus, perhaps this will give you the opportunity to consider the affect your reviews have had on other filmmakers and myself. With that thought in mind, from this book, maybe all of us will become more conscious and invoke a more caring process of human interaction, realizing that everything everyone does has a wide spanning effect and the artist and the creative person can never truly be judged by anyone but themselves. Like I always say, *"Think about the other person first before you do anything that may affect anyone."* Mostly, hopefully you, the reader, can have some fun reading these reviews. But remember, don't take them too seriously.

As my motto always has been, *"Be Positive."* Have fun with these reviews and see them for they are: the positive, the negative, the truthful, the distorted, and the lies. And remember, if you weren't there, you weren't there. Not being there means you have absolutely no firsthand knowledge about anything that took place.

Remember, what is the number one rule of Zen Filmmaking? *"Having fun is what it is all about."*

Read on and have fun!

Today
23/Feb/2020 06:35 AM

Today, do something nice for someone.

Do something caring, thoughtful, helpful, or kind.

Do something nice for someone and watch how everybody's everything gets just a little bit better.

Today, tell someone you have hurt that you are sorry.

Tell someone you are sorry even if you are not.

It you can fix the damage you created in their life, do so.

Apologize and watch how everybody's everything gets just a little bit better.

* * *

21/Feb/2020 12:59 PM

The person who is young makes excuses.

The person who is old apologizes.

The Holy Man Circuit
21/Feb/2020 08:16 AM

For anyone who has ever studied an advanced system of physical movement such as the martial arts or yoga you will appreciate that every teacher you study under has a somewhat different approach to teaching based upon their own unique understanding of their body methodology. Yes, they may be teaching the same system but each instructor has a unique approach to presenting that information.

In fact, this is a very good thing. From this, the student practitioner may learn new and unique methods to encounter the art and from this come away as a more evolved practitioner.

Just as a person who studies under various teachers of a physical art becomes more exposed to the wide-spanning understanding of that art, so too is the case with the person who is exposed to the various teaching of the mental arts.

Once upon a time, in the long ago and the far-far away, rising human consciousness was on the minds of many people here in the West. Particularly in large cities like Los Angeles, there was an ongoing procession of spiritual teachers presenting their teachings. Some of these lectures took place in large lecture halls, while others were in living rooms, parks, or bookstores. For those of us who cared about such things it was a great time. You could hear individual teachers presenting their own unique understanding about the pathways to rising consciousness.

For me, it was great time. I felt like I had the opportunity to be exposed to so much positive teaching.

I don't know that the world, or its people, were really any different back then. It was simply a time in history when if you were looking for that kind of thing, it could be easily found.

I remember I got to be friends with this one girl during this period of time. She was one of those people who had gotten married young, the marriage didn't work out, and as she was in the midst of a painful split, she was kinda lost and looking for something more. I gave her some books, took her to some functions, hung out with her, and talked to her about what I was thinking. At least for a time, she seemed to be a bit happier.

One evening, we went to a Frank Zappa concert together. Afterwards we went to one of those Hollywood parties where all of the (then) stars and shiny happy people were hanging out. Cocaine was the drug of choice back then and, of course, the host of the party was walking around with a big tray of the blow. He offered my friend some (who was friends with him) and she, of course, powered her nose. Then, he came to me, *"No thanks."*

In my life, I have very few times ever encountered someone who was so insistent on me doing drugs with them. But, I stood strong. (At least on that occasion). I mean, there I was, I was wearing a pair of white, what are now called yoga pants, Birkenstocks, and prayer beards around my neck. What did he think I was about?

The reason I tell this story is that, even at that time in history, when rising consciousness was on the minds of so many people—and it was so available, the vast majority of the everyone, even those who were young, did not really care. For them, sure, they may acknowledge spiritual reality, reference it from time to time, maybe even take a yoga class, but what their life was really about was rubbing elbows with the cool, rich, and famous, being at the place to be, and getting high.

Eventually, the guy, very disapproving of me, moved along. I think my friend may have been a bit embarrassed with me or disappointed in me. But, my focus was pure.

Time went on and I lost touch with her. I wonder where she is now? But, this is the thing about life and about life's reality; everything changes, everything moves on. Though this is the case, if you are not basing your life on a very specific positive principle then you are lost to the tides of human influences and human influencers. There are always going to be those people out there who attempt to point you down a non-positive road. They are going to be friendly, they are going to be insistent, they may even be deceitful in their attempt to get you to do what they want you to do. But, if you are not firm in a spiritually positive system of belief then you will end up doing things that will hurt your own body, mind, a future, and possibly hurt other people's body, mind, and future.

You need to ask yourself, Who are you? What are you? What are you willing to do? And, why are you willing to do it?

People believe all kinds of things as they pass through their life. Most people do not care about the damage they do to themselves or to others until it comes back to bite them in the ass. They only want to do what they want to do. They only want other people to do what they want them to do based upon their own preconceived notion of reality and what they consider to be right. But, if what you do hurts yourself or anyone or anything, how can that be right? If what you offer people can kill them, how can that be good, even though, for a moment, it may make them feel elated.

Though times have changed and the available reference points have shifted, the truth of life has not changed at all. People are people. People seek a deeper knowledge. People seek the drug of illusion. This is particularly the case when their life is not traveling in the direction they had hoped. So, who are you? What are you? What are you going to do today to put your life on a higher plane of consciousness? What are you going to do today to help anyone else put their life on a higher plane of consciousness? Are you going to offer them a tray of coke or are you going to offer them a plate of enlightenment?

When It All Comes Together
20/Feb/2020 01:58 PM

I was cruising down the street today. I was listening to the great band, *Dengue Fever* on the car stereo. I pulled up to one of those three way lights. And, you know how every now and then everything just comes together. That's what happened. They were doing some road construction over to one side and the blink of the yellow construction lights on the sawhorse thingy was in perfect time with the beat of the music. There was this weird looking guy with his ear buds in, over on one corner, waiting for the light to change, with his head bouncing to his music but in perfect time with mine.

Whenever those things happen, I always wonder if it is nature reminding us how we are all part of the same puzzle. ... That we are all in tune and intertwined.

I sat there listening to the music, relishing in that moment of perfection for a time. Then, my light turned green. Just as I was about to step on the gas, I notice this old guy on a bicycle riding through the intersection. His light was red but he was going anyway. Just then, this other old guy in his junky red 1980s something pickup truck drives right in front of the guy riding his bike. He too had a red light, but he was going anyway. He cut the guy on the bike off but didn't even notice that he had done anything wrong. He just kept driving. The guy on the bike is cussing him out and flipping him off. He looks at me. Me... My moment of interactive perfection gone. But, then the guy on the bike starts shaking his head—shacking his head like I am supposed to understand his frustration. Shaking his head in perfect rhythm to the music.

Sometimes everything just comes together.

The Things You Used To Be
20/Feb/2020 07:03 AM

Back in the days when poetry chapbooks were still the thing I used to do my bio as, *"Former Swami, Former Punk Rocker, Former Ph.D."* It was my way of saying I had moved on.

Have you moved on in your life?

Who were you yesterday that you are not today?

How have you evolved?

Have you evolved?

Many people spend their existence locked into the projection of who they think they are. Many people spend their existence locked into the projection of who other people think they are. Many people spend their existence locked in the projection of a lie of who they want people to believe that they are. In all of these cases, these projections are never who the person truly is, they are simply a fabrication of the mind.

We are all born and defined by where we find ourselves at birth. We are all defined by our family and our socioeconomic standing. We are all defined by the friends we choose. Mostly, we are all defined by the choices we make. What choices have you made?

People move though their life either with a desire to achieve or a desire be unseen and merge with the greater whole. Once that initial choice is made it sets a person on a course of realization—the realization of their desired goal. Each step a person takes on this pathway sets an untold number of karmic repercussions into motion defined by who and what is affected by each step the individual takes.

Each choice in life equals the next available choice. Each accomplishment equals the next available action. Each failure equals the dues that must be paid. But, within all of this there is personal definition.

Is an accomplishment truly an accomplishment if it is no longer a desired end goal? Is a failure truly a failure if it opens up a new understanding about who you truly are?

What we are is what we are. What we have to work with is what we have to work with. But, who we become and what we remain is all a personal choice. You can be what you once were. You can be what you always were. Or, you can become the new and better you at any stage of your life. Your choice.

Are you who you used to be or are you a new you?

* * *
20/Feb/2020 07:03 AM

Everything you collect will have to do be disposed of by somebody else when you die.

Buy Me a Ticket
19/Feb/2020 01:16 PM

I received an interesting invitation from one of my female, *"Friends,"* via one of the social websites. It said, in part, *"You should really come and visit me in Berlin. I know you would love it here."* My reply, *"Why?"* Answer, *"Because I think you are a very interesting person and I would really like to get to know you. I can buy you a ticket if you want."*

All this made me smile. My first thought was to reply, *"You know, I only fly first class."* But, of course, the wisdom of age won out and I said nothing…

All of this set me to thinking about a time a long time ago. I had met this girl in Bangkok and we had one of those great, very passionate, short-lived, love affairs. I had to get back to L.A. to record an album so I left her with tears in her eyes. Several months later I was hanging out in Manila and I got a telex from the girl, telling me she really needed to see me and she would buy me a ticket to Bangkok. Okay, what the hell… Why not?

To make a long story short, I got to Bangkok and I found out a lot of unsavory details about the girl who had basically lied to me about a whole lot of stuff. I broke it off. The next day comes an early morning call to my hotel room. It was the travel agent who had sold the girl my ticket. She was waiting downstairs in the lobby. The girl had not actually paid for the ticket, so the travel agent came collecting. Ultimately, it was me who had to pay for my free ticket. Nothing is free in this world.

Whenever someone wants to meet me for some undisclosed reason, it always makes me wonder why. As I have so often realized, (and stated many times), everyone seems to want something from me but nobody ever gives me anything. That's just the condition of my life, I guess.

What I have observed over the years is that when people ask for a meeting, and I decline, then all of a sudden they hate me.

I get some stupid insulting response. But, is the person who declined the invitation any different from the person who received it? Again, that person is not taking me, the human being, into consideration. And, what do I have to offer anyone anyway?

If I would have received this request from that woman when I was in my twenties, I would have probably seen it as some kind of sign and I would have hopped over there straight away. Now, in my sixties, I just have to question, why? It is not that the wanderlust has left me, it is just that I have realized through time and through life experience that nothing is free and there is always a price to pay.

When Things Go Wrong
19/Feb/2020 07:45 AM

Though there is a lot of social commentary in the movie *Forrest Gump,* I think one of the most fun scenes is when the central charter is interacting with a guy who is encountering some problems and he nonchalantly says, *"Shit happens."* This is one of the common threads for all of our lives. Things are going along fine and then something occurs, and as small of a situation as it may be, to us it is a major incident and we get very upset.

Look at your life. You are most probably reading this piece as you sit in front of your computer screen or as you are on your phone. You are probably living a fairly good, fairly safe life. Hopefully, everything is great in your life. Or, maybe there is some small something going on that you are not happy with. You can also think about a time in your life when something was not going as you hoped. Some small thing that derailed your positive thinking and your living life the way you wanted to live your life. Remember how upset you became. Maybe this state of upset caused you to yell, scream, break things, punch the wall, or be mean to others. Maybe you just internalized your upset but it radiated from within you. You were upset. It was your life. But, did anyone else really care?

Now, step back from yourself and look at that situation. Who else's life did it, does it affect? In most cases, those elements of upset that happen to all of our lives maybe have a small rippling effect onto the others who we know, but it is generally only us who experiences the sense of frustration and anger.

When you are locked in those moments, do you ever look outside of yourself? As a human being do you ever include the life and the feelings of others in your thoughts? For most, in these times of life going wrong, people become very selfish. The get lost in the anger they are feeling and the blame they are casting. How about you?

As stated, right now, you are most probably reading this piece as you sit in front of your computer screen or as you are on your phone. Your life is not too bad. This is what you need to think about when those times of things going wrong are happening to you. Yeah, you may be pissed off in your moment. But, that moment will pass. It is not going to last. You should not let it cause you to instigate actions that may have the potential of harming your life or the life of others motivated by the temporary feelings you are feeling.

Look at the world. There is heavy stuff going on. There are some people encountered very-very negative situations every day of their life. That is probably not the case with you. Remember that! Sure, that thing you are upset about may be messing with your head. Yes, you may be very upset that it happened at all. Yes you may be angry at the person or persons who caused it to happen. But, your life is more than that situation. You are more than situation. Instead of being angered by it, instead of letting it control your emotions, take control and do something positive about it. Make it better. Make your life better. And, maybe in the process your can also take your mind off of your Self of a moment and get out there and do something good for someone else.

Shit happens. It happens to all of us. None of us want it to happen. But, when it does happen choose to be the bigger, better person. Learn from it and maybe do something good for someone else because of it.

The Bully of the Bully
18/Feb/2020 03:49 PM

In recent years there has been a lot of talk about online bullying. The classic scenario of bullying is that someone who is bigger or older or has a gang to back him up accosts a younger, weaker individual. I grew up in the hood and this style of behavior when on all the time.

As the internet took over the world, online bullying has come to center stage. We all have heard stories about people who have been hurt or have even taken their own life because of online bullying. Though the person who is doing the bullying no longer has to be bigger or older or have a gang to back them up, they still prey upon those who are in a vulnerable position.

The fact is, most bullies will never go face-to-face, toe-to-toe with the person they are bullying unless they have a crew behind them. This is why so many people have been allowed to get away with it on the internet. Here, anyone can say anything and they won't get punched in the face for having said it.

I never liked the term bullying. It is really too abstract. It make it sound like some big guy is descending upon some little guy. But, that is no loner the case, particularly in this day and age. It is some person off there in cyberspace deciding to hurt the life of some other person for some self-concocted reason and the person they are hurting has no recourse because it is all taking place online.

Last night, this one in-shape, (probably could fight), male TV host was discussing how he had been brutally bullied online over this one really minor and stupid male macho incident that took place years ago. But, like so many others, he could do nothing about it as it all happened out there in the void of the internet.

Any person who becomes somebody, does, or created anything steps to the forefront, as they have become known. They become easy targets. No matter the truth of any of the accusations or attacks a bully unleashes, it doesn't even matter because there are so many lost people out there with nothing better to do then to relish in the attack.

For me, though never a fun experience, I have always attempted to stay philosophic about any online bullying when it has happened to me. I certainly don't like it but I do this because I have witnessed through time the people who behave in this manner always eventually seem to create their own demise. Some, sooner than others.

I remember this martial art guy who used to go around the internet attacking me, (and other practitioners), saying I had bad technique and stupid stuff like that. He ran one of those posting websites for a minute and anytime anybody tried to dispute his claims about me he would disavow their posts or remove them. This is the perfect example of online bullying because how can you fight back when you can't fight back? As time when on and the possibilities of the internet grew, he began to post himself performing martial art techniques. When I saw them I could not help but laugh. He was terrible! And, he spoke terrible Korean when naming his techniques.

That is the perfect example of the bully; especially online. The person who is not very good at something but they want to attack others. What happened to the guy? I don't know. I guess he just fell prey to his own negativity. His website and him fell off the map years ago.

Most people have been kind to me online, but I have experienced other online bullying attacks over the years. In each case, I could not help but wonder why did they bother? What did they gain by hurting my life? But, I guess that also goes to the definition of bullying, a bully bullies because they can get away with it, because they take joy in causing pain to the life of others.

A lot of people say, *"Just be nice."* Me too. You may love what a person says or does or you may hate what a person says or does but if what they are doing is not hurting anyone, why attack them because all that makes you is a bully and bullies always eventually fall.

As human beings, being in the out and about, we are all going to encounter all kinds of things all kinds of ways. Hopefully, no one will ever bully you or say hurtful or untruthful things designed to damage your life. But, the fact is, there is no wide spanning remedy for this style of behavior because the people who do behave in this fashion gain misdirected internal power from their actions and once instigated they are not internally strong enough or even willing to admit that they are wrong. Then, there are the people who join in as a method to take away the humdrum of their life. This too provides the bully with empowerment. Remove all of this and what are they? How many bullies have you seen who walk alone?

Now, many a bully attempts to turn the tables on those who are on the receiving end of their actions. But, there is one sourcepoint to look for whenever a bully is called out and they deny the fact of what they are doing. That is, who instigated what? Who started the something? Who threw the first blow? Who unleashed the initial hurt? The source is always the bully. They did something that targeted someone else. Never let them turn the tables on the truth. A person who is defending themselves is never the bully.

All this being said, there are those of us who care about other people. There are those of us who want to hurt no one. There are those of us who want no one to hurt. There are those of us who want to help everyone we can. There are those of us who decidedly walk a higher path. For us, we must be the voice for the bullied. We must stop the hurt.

Yes, internet bullying is a ridiculous concoction. But, it is definitive of the age in which we live. So, what should we do when we witness it occurring? The answer: meet negativity with positivity. Someone is saying something negative, say something nice. Counteract the hurt and change the direction of the conversation.

And, to all you bullies out there: physical or online, stop it! Be big enough, be strong enough to stop instigating the hurt!

Everybody Keeps Getting Younger
18/Feb/2020 08:25 AM

It is certainly no secret that everybody wants to stay young forever. Everyone is locked into this mindset that youth is somehow more of a something than age. Mostly, many believe it is more desirable. I mean, I get it, youth is beautiful. …Youth meaning a young adult, not a weird pedophilia thing. That's just sick. But, whatever the cause or the case it seems that everybody does all they can to not get old—whether it is dying their hair, getting a face peel, Botox injections, face lifts, trying to dress with the youthful trends, equaling dressing younger than you should, you name it… One of the main things that people do is that they lie about their age.

Having been in the film game for quite awhile now, I have watched this age thing from a firsthand perspective. One of the things that has confounded me over the years is that people keep getting younger. Like if I am watching TV or listening to the radio or something and they spit out a person's age, sometimes I can't help but say, *"Wait a minute, that's not right. They were my age (or older) back then, now all of a sudden they are younger than me. How is that possible?"* Then you check on Google or Bing and their age has been changed. How did they do that? They must have been twelve when they did that movie…

In the film game, there has always been this five-year thing. What people do is to decrease their age by five years. I have even had friends that have done this to me. All along our friendship I thought they were like five or six years younger than me but, as it turns out, they were my age. Not cool. You don't lie to friends!

I think when you are getting to know a person, one of the first questions you ask is how old are they. The answer gives you an idea about their placement in life and perhaps what they have or have not experienced. But, if everyone lies, what are you left with?

I guess it is not a bad thing to want to be young forever. Don't we all wish to remain young and beautiful? But, it also is not realistic. Mostly, if you cannot embrace the age that you are, if you cannot move through life and associate with people from your same age group, (as you want to appear younger by hanging out with the younger crowd), all you become is dishonest. Dishonesty is never a good thing because all it creates is lies built upon lies. Even more important, does any lie you tell in association with your age change who you really are?

Think of all the bad face-lifts out there. Think about the people who have ruined their face trying look younger. Think about all of the lies that have been told in association with age. What does any of that equal? All it equals is a lie. If you cannot be honest all you ever are is a liar. Does anybody really want to hang out with a liar even if they do believe that you are younger than you actually are?

The People Who Don't Understand Are The Ones Who Criticize
17/Feb/2020 01:57 PM

I was listening to a man on the radio today discussing the difference between Hill Country Blues and the Delta Blues. He detailed it as the Delta Blues follow a standardized 1 4 5 pattern where Hill Country Blues follows a much more unconventional song structure. I feel like that was a good definition and it got me to thinking... Whenever anyone asks me who my guitar playing influencers are, I always say, *"Ravi Shankar."*

Now certainly, we all understand that Ravi Shankar played the sitar, not the guitar, but how he influenced me was that through his music I realized that within any stringed instrument you did not have to follow a structured protocol. You could move the tuning, the key, the tempo, and the time signature any way you wished. This is where new and unexplored evolutions of music could be found.

When you listen to the early recordings of Ravi Shankar he played a very traditional raga. As time evolved and the 1960s came upon us, however, he became the ultimate master of free flowing string based instrumentation. His mastery of creating and moving sound was unparalleled. Did everyone like him? No. He too had his critics. But, for anyone with an ear for advanced music execution, there are few musicians that met his unparalleled standard.

After I listened to the discussion about the Blues, I went back to this CD I had in the deck of car. I recently pulled it out of my massive CD collection on a whim.

Side Note here: Very similar with the end of the original Vinyl era, as CDs have progressively gone away, so much unique music has been lost and it may never be found again. So much music that never found mainstream or even cult popularity has just been forgotten.

Back to the story...

I was listening to this CD from a relatively obscure band, *Laterna*. They are an instrumental band, based around the guitar. To describe this CD, I would say that it has a very 1970s guitar feel to it. Very melodic with some nice guitar work.

Listening, it made be think about the free-formed basis of the later musical compositions of Ravi Shankar and the more structure based work of this band, *Laterna.*

People always seem to love structure. Even the people who like the weird or the abstract like that work to be structured. In structure, they find the expected—they find conformity. Once one steps outside of this realm of the expected in their art, music, or otherwise, here one encounters the critics. But, who is criticizing what and why? What is their basis?

As an author, as a musician, as a filmmaker I have encountered criticism at every step of the way, both positive and negative. But, what I always realize when someone is critiquing my work, practically from a negative standpoint, is that they do not understand what I am doing or why I am doing it. They are attempting to place their own definition of conformity onto my work. They are trying to make my work fall into the structure that they are comfortable with. But, by doing this they have negated any true realizations they may come upon. They have simply made up their mind that they are not open to anything new or different.

This is the same with every critic who criticizes any creator of art. They want things to be the way they want things to be and when they are not they attempt to tell the world how wrong that creator and/or their art actually is.

We all like what we like and we don't like what we don't like; that's life. For example, many people associate me with Cult Films because I have made several movies that people have defined as such. The fact is, I am not a fan of Cult Films. I do not consider myself a Cult Filmmaker. So, who is right? Those people out there who are casting their judgment on me and attempting to define the style of films I make by telling the world how they view my films or me, the actual filmmaker, who knows how and why I have made each piece of cinema that I have created?

It's important to keep an open mind in life. It's important to not attempt to define everything that you see, read, or hear, by the structure that is already present in your mind. From this, you become free. From this, you allow everyone to encounter life, reality, and art in their own way. By telling anyone how you feel about anything only proves that you do not understand the true motives of the creator. How could you? Be more than that; let the artist be the artist. And, if you are not the one creating your own art, than choose to be silent and let the natural patterns of life flow to their own reasoning by allowing each person to define how they self interpret each representation of art that they encounter.

The Paradox of Complication
16/Feb/2020 08:13 AM

Look around your life. What do you own? What do you think? How do you feel? What do you feel about your life, what you own, what you don't own but desire, how you feel, and what you think?

Look to the life of other people that you know. What do they own? What do they think? What do they feel about their life, what they own, what they don't own but desire, how they feel and what they think?

How much of your life is lived in simplicity? How much of your life is easy? How much of your future have you designed to be tranquil and free? How much of your life and your future have you set up to be complicated?

People surround themselves with complications. They do thing that will complicate their future. They do these things without giving them a second thought. In fact, if someone tells them they are making their life complicated they will most probably deny this fact.

People buy things on credit. Meaning, they will be paying for those items for a long time, probably incurring interest.

People fall into relationships where they encounter complications. Once they are in them, breaking free may be very hard.

People believe that they are right and someone else is wrong and from this they say and do things that hurt the life of other people, thereby defining their own future by the hurt they have unleashed.

People look to complicated religions to find a purpose and someone or something to thank or blame as they pass through their life. Due to their beliefs they must then attend a church to have their religion translated for them. Thus, they must pay for the life and the lifestyle of that person who is providing them with that translation. But, simply because a person claims to know about religion—simply because they claim that they have the key to the translation between god to man, how are they truly any different from anyone else except for the claims that they are making?

Think about a life where you owed no money for the things you purchased. Think about a life where you did not quest for some desired goal. Think about a life where your relationships were not the dominant force in your existence. Think about a life where you did not judge and hurt no one. Think about a life where no one judged or hurt you. Think about a life where you did not believe that someone else knew god and his wishes more than you. How free would you be?

People choose to make their life complicated. But, it is just as easy to choose to make your life uncomplicated. Your life, your choice.

Let go and be free.

Finding Your Space for Meditation
15/Feb/2020 04:33 PM

Most people, (rightly), believe that meditation is a time to silence their mind. They believe that they must quiet their mind and turn it off from thoughts. All true.

Mediation has always been demonstrated to be a time where the practitioners sits down, in some quite space, and through varying techniques, enters into a state tranquility. Though the idea of meditating is pretty much cemented into the minds of everyone, the practically of actually meditating is a bit more difficult to actualize for many. There is noise from the outside world where many people live or hope to practice meditation. There are distractions of all sorts. From this many people who could find a new understanding of Self and encounter a calmer mind give up on its practice, as it is too difficult to actualize.

The first thing to understand is that meditation does not have to only be performed in seated lotus position. Throughout the centuries many groups and numerous teachers have developed new ways to meditate that do not only involve attempting to turn off the mind in a seated posture. The Sufis have their dances. The Zen Buddhists have, *"Kinhin,"* walking meditation. Onto modern teachers like Bhagwan Shree Rajneesh who taught, *"Dynamic Meditation."* In each of these methods and many more the practitioner is taught that meditation does not have to simply witness the person attempting to sit down and turn off their mind.

As a young adolescent I too believed that meditation could only be performed by sitting down and closing my eyes. But, via being open to new methods and meeting and joining such groups as The Sufi Order I quickly came to learn that meditation could truly take place anywhere. One simply had to be open enough to understand this fact and allow personal circumstances to be the guide in charting that new pathways towards meditation.

For me, one of the first places I developed a new and unique space to meditate was in the shower. A little weird, I get it, but throughout my high school years I lived in this apartment in Hollywood. I had the back bedroom where there was an adjoining bathroom. There was a small shower in this bathroom. I found that if I closed the curtains and closed all the doors it was completely dark in bathroom; no light came through. As it was an apartment, with I guess a gigantic water heater hidden somewhere in the building, the water never got cold and the sound of the shower would drowned out the outside noise. I would close off everything, turn on a warm shower, soap up, wash my hair and stuff, then when I was done with that I would flip off the light, sit down on the floor of the shower, and with the warn water running over me allow my mind to find its way to higher consciousness. Not only was it a very pleasant experience, it was very meditative. And, that is one of the main components that I believe must be present for a person to actually find a positive pathway to meditation, a pleasant experience.

Certainly, throughout time, meditation has been taught as a discipline. There are, of course, all the stories of the sadhus doing all kinds of crazy stuff proving what a holy being they are by forcing their mind to meditate in terrible conditions. But, most people aren't like that. They are not willing to put their body and their mind through those kind of trials and tribulations to meditate. They need a safe, comfortable space where they can naturally drift into meditation.

If you want to meditate, if you want to find that eternal peace and the expansive mind space, you do not have to force yourself to try to meditate in the traditional manner. Be open; be willing to encounter meditation where you find it. Allow yourself to meet your meditative mind wherever you may be, whenever you find a space that will naturally allow you to flow into meditation.

You don't have to follow the rules to meditate. You can be the creator of your own meditation. Allow yourself to find the silence in your mind wherever your encounter that space and meditation no longer has to be a forced chore, it can become a joy.

*　　*　　*

15/Feb/2020 08:07 AM

A miracle happening in your life does not have to be some grand, awe-inspiring event. It can be as simply as you waking up and realizing that your life is not that bad.

Get Into The Moment With Me
14/Feb/2020 09:14 AM

I was eating lunch in a restaurant the other day and across from me were two young men. What they were doing was they had one of their phones leaning up against the wall and they were playing one of those kill or be killed video games. They each had little controllers in their hands and they were going at it. I'd actually never seen that type of situation take place in a restaurant before. Interesting... Two people focused on the same entity yet attempting to overcome one another as participants in a game. Interactive, yet separate.

How many times have you sat down with a person in a restaurant (or anywhere) and instead of them having a conversation with you they bury their head in their phone? Do you do this? You are together with someone but instead of spending that time in human interaction your mind is lost somewhere else.

This is nothing new. Forever one could see couples sitting at the same table, each lost in the newspaper that lay in front of them. Go to any coffee house and people from the old school are lost reading their books while others are locked onto the screen of their computer. What none of these people are, is in the moment. They have cast their mind somewhere else, living some reality that is not directly in front of them, and does not actually exist.

To vary degrees we all do this. Even when you are conversing with a person, your mind is not their mind, and their mind may be interpreting the current situation in a much different way than your mind does. You are speaking but you are thinking how you are going to respond to their statement just as they are thinking about how they are going to respond to yours.

Though living in the, *"Now,"* has been propagated as one of the ultimate states of human consciousness since the dawning of the New Age, there really is no such thing. But, what there is are two or more people being in the same space of consciousness and living their moment together as consciously as possible. They are where they are. They are interactive. They are observing. They are a participant. What they are not, is living in some spaced out frame of mind where all thoughts are on what is going on in some abstract reality that has nothing to do with the now right in front of them—right in this moment.

People seek escape from the moment they are living for many reasons. People create excuses for casting their mind somewhere else all the time. Maybe they even believe that they should be doing something else than living what they are living. But, if you are not living what you are living to its fullest, if you are not experiencing your moment to the best of your ability, if you are not as fully interactive with the person who is in front of you as possible, what you have done is to diminish your moment and cast it to the realm of the unimportant. If you do this, the beauty of that moment has been dismissed, anything you can learn from that moment has been lost, and any truthful human interaction you could have encountered is gone forever.

People seem to continually forget that life is lived in the moment. Your moment is all you have because once that moment is gone it is gone. It will never happen again. If you don't live your moment(s) to their fullest, if you cast your mind to somewhere else that is not real, than all you will be left with is a life unlived, cast to a false reality that doesn't really matter.

The Precepts of Your Purpose
13/Feb/2020 04:05 PM

I hit over to my local Starbucks this afternoon. As I was walking in I notice a woman in her mid-thirties getting out of her Austin Martin. She was dressed very nice. But, the main thing I noticed about her was she was wearing these very 1990s sunglasses. …You know, small in size. I went around the back of the building to grab an ocean view seat on the patio while my lady ordered our lattes.

The aforementioned woman joined up with her friends, sat down, and immediately lighted up cigarette. Now, for anyone who knows anything, Starbucks is a smoke free zone. Not to mention, smoking is just a disgusting habit. Luckily, the smoke wasn't blowing my direction but it was a busy afternoon, there were a lot of people there, including several kids with their parents sitting around being impacted by this woman's smoking.

As I listened, she was speaking a high dialect of Arabic, so I gave her the benefit of the doubt that maybe she didn't know the rules and the regulations. This, even though there are all kinds of no smoking symbols around the patio. I mean, had the smoke been hitting my direction I would have had to go and talk with the Starbucks people to get it to stop or I would have just left. But, as stated, I was not directly impacted by it.

In the few minutes that passed as I sat waiting for my latte, the woman had gone through three cigarettes. Obviously a chain smoker. But, the problem with a habit like this is, as we all understand, hurting yourself hurts other people. My question is, how can anyone be so uncaring that they allow what they do to impact the life of other people in a negative manner and they do it for no other reason than to quench their developed addition? Selfishness? Nihilism? Power tripping? Or, most probably, just someone who doesn't give a fuck about anyone but themselves—taking no one else into consideration. How many people are like that? How about you?

Anyway, for me, it was all a study in human interaction and human consciousness. And, I think it/this goes to the root cause of all action, positive or negative, that someone/anyone does.

Why do you do what you do? Do you ever deeply contemplate this question? Do you ever spread you psychic feelers out and study how what you do impacts the lives of other people.

The fact is, just like this woman today, most people don't care—they don't give a fuck. All they care about is themselves and how they are feeling in any given moment. As long as their addiction (to whatever) is being met, they are all good. They are all good and everyone else be damned.

If you truly care about others… If you truly care about life… If you truly care about helping and not hurting, you need to take the other person into consideration in everything that you do. If you don't, all you are—all you can ever become is a person who destroys the all and the everything of everybody else which ultimately does nothing but diminish your essence with every breath that you take.

And Then They Don't Remember Your Name
12/Feb/2020 03:43 PM

I always find it curious the way certain people progress towards fame. What many do is to use each person that they can as a stepping-stone towards achieving their end goal and then, if they do achieve fame, they forget that person's name.

Certainly, of all of the people who fight their way towards fame, very few find it. The primary reason for that is that they attempt to enter into a world where there is no control. They attempt to become something abstract such as a, *"Movie Star,"* or something like that. That is a world were so many people have to approve of a person's passageway that there are very few that can find the acceptance to move through the ranks. Thus, many leave behind their dreams of fame very disappointed.

There are other ways towards fame, particularly in this day and age. Now, one with the right focus and dedication can forge their own pathway towards success. Along the way, as stated, they too borrow from and ask for the help of others. When they are in a position of need, they happily take. When they rise to the level when they can return the favor, they forgot all those that they drew from in the first place.

As someone who forged a new pathway in cinema, I have encountered so many people who have asked me for guidance and help along the way. Some have borrowed my methods of creation and adapted them to their own methodology. Some have used my name as a reference. In all of those cases, I have been happy to help in any way that I can. A few of these people have, in fact, risen up in the game but all of sudden they have forgotten my name. They have forgotten where they gained their inspiration. They have forgotten whom they have borrowed what from. Why is this? The answer, success. When they are the one in front of the camera or the microphone why say, *"Thanks,"* any more? They don't need to. Now, all eyes are on them and they want to bask in the glory. And, they certainly do not want to give anyone else any credit for guiding them towards their success. They want it to look like they did it all on their own.

I get it. I get why people behave in this manner. I also understand that is why so many do not understand the true essence of creativity and why so many, once famous people, fall away. What they have not done is to establish their own foundation of creative truth. Instead, all they have done is to borrow someone else's. And, though they may, at least for a moment, become more famous than the person they once felt was a mentor, they have not established their own brand and thus, through time, their success falls away.

For each of us who walk the creative path, we have had our inspirations, our mentors, and our supporters. They are the people who helped us when we were first starting out. They are the people who helped us become what we have become. And, they are the ones who guided or inspired our art in its early stages. If these people are not credited for their inspirational input, what does that make the person who had borrowed and/or build upon what that individual motivated?

We each build upon what we learn from others. Most people simply pass through life with little thought about this fact. Those who pursue fame are doing so in order that they may rise and be acknowledged by the greater masses. Whether the fame they gain is large or small, they are seeking it to place themselves in the forefront of human consciousness. If they cannot or will not credit who has guided them towards their achievements, not only does this make them a false prophet but it diminishes the truth in their art. If they cannot give thanks and provide a source for their inspiration at each juncture of their progression towards fame, then they are not telling their audience the truth. What is someone who does not tell the truth?

For those of us who look to art as a lifestyle, for those of us who appreciate art, for those of us who study art, by whatever form we find it, it is essential that we know the evolution of the artist to truly appreciate what that artist has created. Thus, if an artist cannot continually give thanks to their inspirations then the true essence of their art, the true art of their life, is lost. From this, they become nothing more that a person's seeking ego gratification and accolades. Thus, they are not a true artist at all.

* * *

12/Feb/2020 07:19 AM

Most people look outside of themselves to find excuses for their bad behavior.

* * *
12/Feb/2020 07:17 AM

If you tell a liar, *"Don't lie to me,"* will they stop lying to you?

* * *

12/Feb/2020 06:56 AM

You won't be sent to jail for thinking bad thoughts but bad thoughts will cloud how you encounter life.

Choose to think positive thoughts.

Lingerie Kickboxer and Friends Then and Now
11/Feb/2020 08:31 AM

I was flipping channels on the TV last night, with a glass of the grape in my hand. I came upon the TV Show, *Pawn Stars,* just when someone had brought in a supposed first printing copy of the comic book, *Teenage Mutant Ninja Turtles.* Knowing the co-creator of that comic book, I stopped flipping the channels. Low-and-behold, a couple of minutes later they brought in Kevin Eastman, the co-creator, as the expert as to its authenticity.

It was good to see him again. We haven't hung out in years, though I do have his cell number in my phone. A little bit grayer, a little bit heavier, but still the same nice-guy. Hey, we all get older…

Seeing him and them referencing the first printing copy of the comic book got me to remembering one of the movies we did together, *Lingerie Kickboxer.* One of the main pay offs of the film was that these lingerie clad kickboxer thieves were attempting to steal Kevin's copy. That was a long time ago, 1998, and a movie that will probably never see the light of day. You can read some of the backstory about it on the *Lingerie Kickboxer* page on this site if you want.

But, more than just the memory of the shoot, it got me to thinking about Hollywood, the Film Game, and how there are so many things that go on behind the scenes that even the people involved don't really know about. I mean, Julie Strain (Kevin's then wife) got Entertainment Tonight to come to the set and do a story about the film. …She must have had one major publicist back then as why the hell would *Entertainment Tonight* come to a low-budget set if she just told them that Scott Shaw, Don Jackson, and some porn stars were going to be there?

…I have a copy of the broadcast of that ET piece. Though the focus is solely on Julie, there is a glimpse of Don and I. I should put it up on my YouTube channel along side that Behind the Scenes piece I did on the film after finding some lost footage of the movie a year or so ago.

It was kind of funny, (or whatever you want to call it), but Julie had sold herself as the director of the movie to ET. This pissed Don off beyond belief, as it was to be a three-person directed piece. Look at the poster Kevin and Simon Bizely created to confirm this fact. Anyway, prior to ET coming to the set, I actually Faxed (Remember those) them the backstory about the fact that LKB was based on my original concept and that Don and I were also the directors. But, that equaled nothing. The ET piece focused on Julie. Like I say, she must have had a major publicist in play.

We finished the movie. I edited it. Julie and Kevin came up with a few fixes they wanted to do—all of which would have cost big-big money. But, that never happened. I few months later, Julie offered to buy the rights of the film from Don and I. $3,000.00 per... For me, it was a god-sent as my Porsche had broken down and it was right at 3G's to get it out of the shop.

Don and I took the checks Julie had written to us over to her bank in Beverly Hills, where we bumped into Little Richard, cashed them, and that was that. The movie was lost forever.

If I still had the rights, you know me, I would have completed it, sound tracked it, and released it. But, now it is lost in Hollywood Never-Never-Land.

I doubt that it would have made any money, most indie films never do. But, that never-out-there illusion has made a lot of people over the years wish to see it.

But, that's the thing, life and people move on. Some you remember with fond memories, like I have for Julie and Kevin, others, not so much...

Last night, just before watching that segment of Pawn Stars, I was discussing with my lady how this one so-called, *"Friend,"* had convinced me to sell this guitar that held a lot of sentimental value for me several years ago. You know, we all need money to survive, and he made it sound like he was getting me major top dollars for it. I said, "Yes," when I should have said, *"No."* Later, I found out that I could have gotten upwards of a hundred thousand dollars for that guitar. Which is nowhere near what I got. That money would have changed my life. The money he got me, did not.

Here's the thing, I don't really see Julie or Kevin anymore, but all I have is good feelings towards them. Sure, LKB is probably lost forever, but the fun we had making that movie and her hooking Don and I up with some money to bury it; all good!!!

I don't see that other, *"Friend,"* anymore either… That's more of a choice. I just don't have good feeling about him and what he did…

So, as the story goes, what are you doing now to and for your, *"Friends?"* How is what you are doing with them and for them going to affect their memory of you? And, if they see you years later, a little grayer and a little heavier, are they going to remember you with fond memories?

Think about what you do. Think about how it will affect your memory in the mind of others. Think about how people will feel about you years down the line…

Do what you do with this thought in mind and you will be remembered fondly.

Self-Empowerment Verse Desired Dominance
10/Feb/2020 07:55 AM

    Some people evolve into a life position possessing a strong sense of self-awareness where they find their life moving in a positive direction towards self-fulfillment. Other people must struggle and fight to make themselves feel like that are strong, powerful, and in control individual. The difference between these two mindsets is vast and it manifests in many ways. The person who is struggling to find an interpersonal sense of empowerment, however, often times walks down an unhealthy road attempting to make others see and appreciate their sense of self-worth which often times comes off as aggressive, combative and, from this, leads them down the roads towards possible disaster.

    I was in a store in Hollywood, purchasing a new tripod, over the weekend. This store has a large parking lot. The problem is, (I guess), is that there are other businesses and restaurants around the area where people snake parking spots from this store. In any case, I had walked out to my car. After I put the tripod in my truck, I looked around a bit. As I did, I see this one employee gawking at me from across the parking lot. He was giving me one of those hard stares. Whatever... As I am driving out of the parking lot he confronts me near the driveway. *"This is not a public parking lot! You can't park here!"* Somewhere between amused and pissed off, I pull out my receipt, *"I just bought something."* Unphased, *"This is not a public parking lot! You can't park here!"* *"What's your name,"* I inquire. *"Joseph."* My response, *"Fuck you, Joseph."* I drive away.

    Now, here was a situation that had no reason for occurring. I was a customer. I had even made an expensive purchase. But, here was some guy, attempting to exhibit his own self of self-worth, and project his empowerment onto others.

    I believe we have all encountered people who behave like this. ...People who feel they have the power, should have the power, and then express their self-envisioned power. Of course, this style of behavior is based in a sense of insecurity and a lacking sense of self worth. But, it virtually all cases, it leads to unnecessary conflict and a worsening of expansive reality.

You see this kind of nonsense on the internet all the time. People attempting to empower themselves by telling other people what is right, wrong, or otherwise. As there are no checks and balances on the internet, anybody can say anything about anybody or anything. Right or wrong, truth or a lie, it does not even matter.

The problem is, all this style of self-activated empowerment does is to create an environment of conflict, where wars can break out. And, from this, all that occurs is damage but nothing good.

Maybe the person who does not possess a strong sense of Self may make themselves feel like they are stronger or a part of the bigger whole. But, are they? Or, are they simply a person who has added to the further pain and chaos of a world already in crisis?

Virtually, anyone who does anything can claim that they have a reason for doing what they do. If it is done to help or if it is done to hurt doesn't even matter. They feel like they are doing something and from that doing it gives them a sense of purpose. I assume Joseph thought he was doing something for his employer that he believed would get him Brownie Points. But, all his implementation did was to create conflict and if he did what he did to the wrong person he may have ended up with a fist in his face.

Here's the thing… Who are you? Who are you inside? How do you feel about yourself inside of your being? And, what does that feeling cause you to do?

Are you aware of who you are inside? Are you aware of what your feeling about yourself causes you to do?

The very simply formula for living a good life is, if what

you are doing (or about to do) is going to cause conflict—if it is going to hurt anybody, don't do it. Because just like in the case of Joseph, what he did equaled nothing but negativity. He didn't become more empowered. Somebody just told him, *"Fuck you."*

*   *   *

10/Feb/2020 07:55 AM

Sometimes if you tell someone who or what they are, even if they are not, that is what they become.

* * *

09/Feb/2020 07:11 AM

When you blame someone else for the negative things they have done to your life does that make them look bad for doing what they have done or you look bad for allowing them to do it?

* * *

08/Feb/2020 07:55 AM

Who is the truly bad person?

Answer: The individual who will not admit to themselves that they are a bad person.

THE
ZEN